THE KOREAN WAR

Text by
NIGEL THOMAS
and PETER ABBOTT
Colour plates by
MIKE CHAPPELL

First published in Great Britain in 1986 by
Osprey Publishing, Elms Court, Chapel Way, Botley.
Oxford OX2 9LP, United Kingdom.
Email: info@ospreypublishing.com

Also published as Men-at-Arms 174
The Korean War 1950-53

© 1986 Osprey Publishing Limited
00 01 02 03 04   10 9 8 7 6 5 4 3 2 1

British Library Cataloguing in Publication Data

Nigel Thomas and Abbott, Peter
    The Korean War 1950–53.—(Men-at-arms series; 174)
    1. Korean War, 1950–1953
    I. Title   II. Thomas, Nigel. *1946–*   III. Series
    951.9'042   DS918

    ISBN 1 84176 120 6

Filmset in Great Britain
Printed in China through World Print Ltd.

FOR A CATALOGUE OF ALL BOOKS PUBLISHED BY
OSPREY MILITARY, AUTOMOTIVE AND AVIATION
PLEASE WRITE TO:

The Marketing Manager, Osprey Direct USA,
PO Box 130, Sterling Heights, MI 48311-0130, USA.
Email: info@OspreyDirectUSA.com

The Marketing Manager, Osprey Direct UK,
PO Box 140, Wellingborough, Northants, NN8 4ZA,
United Kingdom.
Email: info@OspreyDirect.co.uk

Visit Osprey at:
www.ospreypublishing.com

FRONT COVER: US troops advancing on Taegu during
the offensive following the Inchon landings in autumn 1950.

BACK COVER: A US Marine squad returning from
patrol - December 1951 (USMC)

Acknowledgements

A work such as this would not have been possible
without the generous help of others. Special thanks
are due to Mike Cox, Shelby Stanton, Y. C. Choe
(Korean Veterans' Association), Lee Russell, and Col.
Arnott (DLI, Ret.). We would also like to thank
Lt.Col. (Ret.) L. Turcott (Royal 22ᵉ Regt.), Ted
Zuber, W. A. B. Douglass (Canadian Defense HQ),
John Scurr, P. J. Burness (Australan War Memorial),
Shaun Bland, Lt.Col. H. L. Zwitzer (Royal Neth-
erlands Army), Pierre C. T. Verheye, J. Ludriksen
(R.No.A.F.), Capt. Togas (Hellenic Navy), Col. M.
S. Okcay (Turkish Army), Office of Military History
USMC, J. Anker Nielsen (Royal Danish Embassy)
and Capt. H. Stradiot (Belgian Navy).

The Course of the War

The Korean peninsula, 450 miles long and averaging 160 miles wide, is about the size of Great Britain or Southern California. Some 3,000 small islands ring the coast; and the Yalu and Tumen Rivers separate it from the People's Republic of China and the Soviet Union. The countryside is mostly forest, and the Taebaek mountain range forms a central spine close to the east coast. In summer there is blinding heat, choking dust and monsoon thunderstorms; in winter, bitter cold.

Korea, the isolated 'hermit kingdom' inhabited by a Buddhist people related racially to the Japanese and Manchurians, was occupied by Imperial Japan after August 1910. In 1943 the Allies promised Korea independence; and in August 1945 Japanese troops north of the arbitrarily chosen 38th Parallel surrendered to Soviet occupying forces, and those in the south to the US Army. Thereafter the Soviet-American 'Cold War' intensified; in August 1948 President Syngman Rhee proclaimed the 'Republic of Korea' ('ROK') on behalf of 21 million South Koreans, followed in September by the declaration of President Kim Il-Sung's Communist 'Democratic Republic of Korea' for nine million North Koreans. Both states claimed sole legitimacy over all Korea, leading to considerable mutual suspicion and border tension.

At 4 am (Korean time) on Sunday 25 June 1950 powerful North Korean forces invaded South Korea, advancing down the Uijongbu Corridor, the historic invasion route, towards the Southern capital of Seoul, in a determined attempt to reunite Korea by force. ROK troops resisted bravely, but were crushed by overwhelming Northern superiority. Later that day the United Nations Security Council condemned the aggression, and on 7 July appointed US General of the Army Douglas MacArthur to command UN forces which would be sent to save South Korea. The Soviet Union, which had been boycotting UN meetings, missed the chance to veto the decision.

Meanwhile, the North Koreans advanced relentlessly southwards; a mob of refugees and disorientated ROK troops fled before them, choking roads already turned into quagmires by the monsoon. On 27 June the invaders took Seoul; on 5 July they

The cotton summer uniform of a North Korean KPA corporal modelled by a Japanese employee of the US Army in July 1953: compare with Plate A1. This is the earlier style, with two pockets and wrist bands. The detachable shoulder boards are olive green, piped red, with gold bars. Note the interesting canvas-and-leather personal equipment. (US Army via Lee Russell)

brushed aside a token force of US troops at Osan; and on 20 July they crushed a more determined stand at Taejon. US reinforcements were now pouring in and, with ROK troops, they established a 200-mile defensive line in south-eastern Korea, around the port of Pusan.

The Battle of the Pusan Perimeter began on 1 August as US forces (now designated the 8th Army) and ROK troops defended an area 80 miles long by 50 miles wide. The North Koreans mistakenly deployed their forces along the entire perimeter instead of concentrating them for a definitive breakthrough. Although they did make some advances, they were always repulsed. On 28 August British troops—the first of many UN contingents— arrived in the perimeter; North Korean pressure eased as UN aircraft bombed their supply-lines, and local peasants withheld food. By 14 September the UN had won the battle, and the initiative now lay with the 8th Army.

On 15 September 1950 a US amphibious force from Japan stormed ashore on the west coast at Inchon, and 11 days later recaptured Seoul against heavy North Korean resistance. Meanwhile, on 16 September, US/ROK troops burst out of the Pusan Perimeter in several directions; a mobile force stormed north-westwards and linked up with US forces at Seoul on the 26th, thereby trapping considerable numbers of enemy troops in the South. By 30 September organised North Korean resistance in South Korea was practically over. Now the UN, after initial hesitation, mandated MacArthur to invade North Korea. UN troops advanced in the west, capturing the North Korean

June—September 1950

September—November 1950

A typically idealised painting showing Kim Il-Sung surrounded by admiring KPA troops.

capital of P'yongyang on 19 October, while ROK forces pressed forward in the east, actually reaching the Chinese border on 26 October. Just as North Korea, her territory now reduced to frontier enclaves in the north-west and north-east, seemed doomed, Chinese forces intervened on 14 October; they counter-attacked strongly in the north-west, forcing the UN advance to a standstill as the cruel North Korean winter began to break.

On 24 November MacArthur launched the final offensive against North Korea; but the very next day his central front collapsed, as massive Chinese forces broke through and advanced southwards. Now UN forces began a fighting retreat through blizzards and across frozen rivers out of North Korea; and it was not until mid-December that they were able to organise a defensive line roughly on the 38th Parallel, where they braced themselves for the expected offensive by Chinese and new North Korean divisions. Meanwhile, UN troops marooned in north-eastern North Korea executed a classic fighting retreat to the coast at Hŭngnam, whence the US Navy evacuated them to South Korea.

The end of 1950 saw the conclusion of this first phase of the war: mobile warfare characterised by spectacular offensives alternating with apparently hopeless retreats. Chinese involvement meant that outright victory was now unattainable for either side, but the prospect of defeat was also unthinkable. As the vast manpower of China confronted the almost unlimited firepower of the United Nations, the conflict degenerated into a static war of attrition centred on the 38th Parallel.

November 1950 – January 1951

July 1953 Ceasefire Line

At dawn on New Year's Day 1951 the Communists attacked all along the front, forcing UN troops back. Seoul was abandoned once more; but on 15 January the front stabilised, in appalling snowstorms, 40 miles south of the capital. On 25 January UN forces began a cautious advance; repelled a Chinese counter-attack on 11 February; and pushed forward relentlessly until 21 April, as exhausted Communist units retreated before them. By late February the thaw had transformed the countryside into a sea of mud, but on 15 March Seoul was retaken once again, and the border into North Korea was crossed. Then, on 11 April, President Truman abruptly dismissed Gen. MacArthur over 'political differences' and appointed Gen. Ridgway as UN/ROK Commander.

On 22 April 1951 the Communists began their 'First Spring Offensive', breaching UN lines in the central sector, and forcing a retreat to a new line north of Seoul. By 30 April the attack was spent, and the UN edged forward before taking the full force of the 'Second Spring Offensive' on 16 May, which again ruptured the central sector, but which was contained after a limited retreat in the east. Now the UN advanced, determined on a strategy to carry the battle into North Korea, but not to attempt another full-scale invasion. By 10 June they had established a line 20 miles above the 38th Parallel, astride the crucial enemy supply and communications centre called the 'Iron Triangle'. On 23 June Jacob Malik, the Soviet Deputy Foreign Minister, proposed a ceasefire; and on 10 July talks opened at Kaesong, in 'No Man's Land' just north of Seoul. In anticipation of an imminent agreement, fighting was restricted to patrolling and local skirmishes; but when talks broke down at the end of August the UN recommenced the offensive, making valuable gains before discussions resumed on 25 October at Panmunjom, near Kaesong.

In November 1951 the war reached its third and final phase—stalemate. While talks continued the UN ceased active operations and maintained a static defence line with minimum casualties, while continuing air attacks on enemy communications and naval bombardment of North Korean ports. On the ground, action was limited to patrolling, regimental-size engagements, and artillery barrages. This continued until May 1952, when the Chinese became more aggressive, escalating their own artillery fire and in June launching an unsuccessful attempt to breach the central sector.

By July 1952 both armies had constructed such strong defensive lines that neither side could undertake a major offensive without incurring unacceptable losses. The Communists therefore sent infantry supported by artillery and tanks against tactically important hills along the UN line in the so-called 'Battle of the Outposts'. These attacks often succeeded initially, but the UN usually retook the hills, although not without significant losses. UN and ROK forces retaliated with surprise raids, and these skirmishes intensified into heavy fighting until the onset of winter brought them to a halt. In March 1953 the 'Final Battles' commenced with a Chinese attack in the west, followed by heavy pressure on the central sector in June and July, forcing UN lines back three miles.

'Socialist realism' in war art: a North Korean painting showing 'valiant KPA soldiers' in hand-to-hand combat with 'brutal imperialists' of the US 7th Division.

Finally, on 27 July 1953, the long-awaited Armistice was signed at Panmunjom, and the three-year-old Korean War was over.

The Armistice left the Western democracies with a sense of anticlimax. North and South Korea were utterly devastated, totally dependent on the USSR or the United States for economic survival. Casualties had been unexpectedly high: 84,000 UN/ROK, 140,000 Chinese and North Koreans, and two million civilians, all dead. And yet the war had brought real achievements and changes. The People's Republic of China took its place as a world power. China and the other Communist states were exposed as aggressive, ruthless, formidable, but not invincible, opponents, breeding in the West a sense of insecurity that led to a strengthening of the NATO alliance (and a reliance on the deterrent effect of nuclear weapons which many believe to be excessive).

South Korean independence had been successfully defended; but this achievement, and the heroism and sacrifice of the UN/ROK forces, now seem to pale before the shining triumphs of the Second World War and the stark tragedy of Vietnam. This continuing sense of anticlimax is preserved today at Panmunjom where, 22 years after the Armistice, the opposing sides still argue about the agenda of the future Peace Conference.

North Korea

One of the guerrilla leaders opposing the 1931 Japanese invasion of China was the young Korean Communist Kim Il-Sung (formerly Kim Sung Chu), who in 1930 had formed the Korean People's Revolutionary Army in China. On 25 April 1932 this combined with other nationalist groups in the Anti-Japanese Guerrilla Amy operating on the Manchuria-Korea border. Captured in 1940, Kim escaped to the Soviet Union in 1941, returning in 1945 as a Soviet Army Major to the Soviet Zone of Korea (already under local nationalist control). By February 1946 Kim and his 150,000-strong People's Militia had taken power; and in September 1948 he became President of the new Democratic People's Republic of Korea.

The KPA—Korean People's Army (Cho-sŏn In-

Lt.Gen. Nam Il (centre) leading the delegation of North Korean and Chinese generals at the Armistice Talks in July 1952: cf. Plate A3 for general characteristics of KPA officers' uniform. As 'volunteers' the green-clad Chinese follows normal P.L.A. practice in Korea in wearing no military insignia.

Min Kun)—was established on 8 February 1948 from former guerrilla units and the Korean Volunteer Corps—Korean Communists in the Chinese People's Liberation Army. By December 1948 Soviet troops had officially left, but 'advisers' remained; while the Maoist guerrilla model was rejected in favour of Soviet military organisation, subversion and border raids continued against South Korea.

In June 1950 the 223,080-strong KPA was organised into ten Infantry Divisions, each with three three-battalion regiments, an artillery regiment (three 12-gun battalions), a self-propelled gun battalion (12 SU-76s) and services, totalling 12,092 men. Some 102,000 served in other units. The KPA order of battle was:

1st Div. (HQ Sinmak) . . . 20, 22, 24 Inf.Regts. (one regt. ex-PLA)

2nd Div. (HQ Wonsan) . . . 4, 6, 17 Inf.Regts.

3rd Guards Div. (HQ Wonsan) . . . 7, 8, 9 Inf.Regts.

4th Div. (HQ Changnyon) . . . 5, 16, 18 Inf.Regts. (one regt. ex-PLA)

5th Div. (HQ Namhung) . . . 10, 11, 12 Inf.Regts. (ex-PLA 164th Div.)

6th Div. (HQ Sariwon) . . . 13, 14, 15 Inf.Regts. (ex-PLA 166th Div.)

7th Div. (HQ Haeju) . . . 1, 2, 3 Inf.Regts. (ex-PLA 139, 140, 141, 156 Div.)

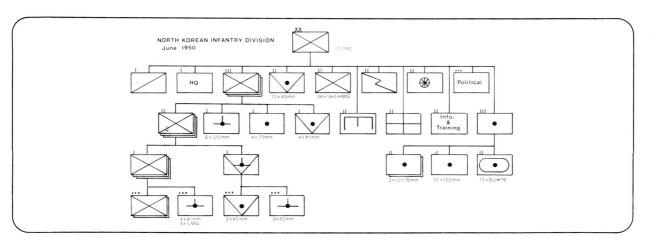

NORTH KOREAN INFANTRY DIVISION
June 1950

10th Div. (HQ Unsanni) . . . 25, 27, 29 Inf.Regts. (formed March 1950)

13th Div. (HQ Chonju) . . . 19, 21, 23 Inf.Regts. (formed June 1950)

15th Div. (HQ Yongdaeri) . . . 45, 48, 50 Inf.Regts. (formed March 1950)

105th Armd.Bde. . . . 107, 109, 203 Regts. 206 Mech.Inf. (each with 40 T-34/85 tanks)

Other units were the 122 mm Artillery Regt. (1,300 men); Anti-Aircraft Artillery Regts. (1,200); 603rd Motorcycle Reconnaissance Regt. (3,500); the Engineer Brigade (2,500); Signal Regt. (1,000); 1st and 2nd Military Academies (4,000); Guerrilla and Commando Forces (2,500); Internal Security (34,000); and other forces (15,700). There was also a Navy (13,700), Air Force (2,000) and Marines (9,000). The Ministry of the Interior controlled the 19,000-strong Border Constabulary (*Bo An Dae*) with five brigades (1-3, 5, 7) each with six to seven battalions, formed from Koreans originally living in the Soviet Union.

The KPA commander was Gen. Choi Yung Kun under the Supreme Commander, Field Marshal Kim Il-Sung. KPA generals were battle-hardened China veterans, skilled in Soviet-style mobile warfare, leading well-armed, disciplined and motivated troops who were initially more than a match for the lightly-armed South Koreans.

For the invasion, seven combat-ready divisions were grouped into a 'Front' (equivalent to a Western Army) under Gen. Kim Chaek, controlling two 'Armies' (Army Corps): 1st Army (1st, 3rd, 4th, 6th Divs., 105th Armd.Bde.), and 2nd Army (2nd, 5th, 7th Divs.). 1st Army swiftly overran the

exposed Ongjin Peninsula and sent 3rd and 4th Divs. and 105th Bde. to occupy Seoul; while 2nd Army advanced in the east, reinforced by 886th Commando and 549th Marine units, and 766th Commando unit landed on the coast behind ROK lines.

After the fall of Seoul the formations were re-organised. 3rd and 4th Divs. each received the honour-title 'Seoul Division', and 105th Brigade became the 105th 'Seoul' Armoured Division, adding the 308th SPG Bn. to its strength. On 2 July 7th Div. was redesignated 12th 'Antung' Div.; 7th Border Bde. was expanded to become the new 7th Div.; 8th Div. was activated; 9th Div. (1st–3rd Border Regts.) was raised from 3rd Border Bde., and 10th, 13th and 15th Divs. were mobilised.

When the seemingly irresistible KPA was finally stopped on the Pusan Perimeter, time began to work against the North Koreans; their over-stretched supply-lines were vulnerable, and their best units were committed on the Perimeter, leaving their homeland dangerously exposed. The 1st Army in the west (2–4th, 6th, 7th, 9th, 10th, 105th Divs.) and 2nd Army in the north (1st, 5th, 8th, 12th, 13th, 15th Divs.) battered the UN lines, but by mid-September their offensive had run out of steam.

The 9th Div. rushed from Pusan to join the 18th Div. and 549th Marines in opposing the Inchon landing; but Seoul soon fell, cutting off supplies to the south. The 1st Army was smashed by US Divs. advancing westwards, while 2nd Army managed to retreat northwards before collapsing. Some units continued to operate as guerrillas in northern South Korea; and 30,000 demoralised stragglers fled into North Korea with US/ROK forces in hot pursuit. A

Weary ROK troops—note extreme youth of soldier at left centre—making their way into British lines after the Chinese breakthrough in the offensive of late 1950. See Plate B. (Imperial War Museum)

temporary defensive line was established to cover P'yongyang with seven divisions including some newly designated formations (9th, 14th, 17th, 18th, 31st, 32nd, 42nd and one other), while three (1st, 249th, and one other) fought in the east; but on 19 October the capital fell, and Kim Il-Sung fled to Sinuiju on the Yalu. The KPA had lost 335,000 men, and the survivors were sheltering on the Chinese border.

Now the Chinese PLA intervened to save North Korea. A Combined Headquarters was established at Mukden, Manchuria, with Kim Il-Sung as nominal Commander-in-Chief but with the Chinese holding the real power. The KPA was re-organised with amazing speed, and by early December there were four armies: in the west 1st Army (105th Armd., 17th, 47th Divs.) and 5th Army (3rd, 4th 7th, 9th 42nd); and in the east 2nd Army (2nd, 6th, 10th, 31st Divs.) and 3rd Army (8th, 18th). Appearances were deceptive, however, for 1st Army, with only 19,800 men, was equivalent to a division. As the rebuilt KPA pushed southwards with the Chinese, 20,000 former 2nd

Army troops operated behind UN lines, disrupting the UN retreat. By the end of 1950 all North Korea had returned to Communist control.

In the 1951 New Year offensive 1st Army (8th, 17th Mech., 47th Divs.) and 5th Army (6th, 7th, 13th, 32nd, 43rd) helped retake Seoul; but the main effort was in the east, opposing less formidable ROK forces. 3rd Army (1st, 3rd, 5th Divs.) stayed in reserve, but 2nd Army (2nd, 3rd, 9th, 10th, 27th, 31st) and 12th Div. broke through, infiltrating guerrillas behind UN lines. 10th Div. penetrated deep into South Korea, and in March, under constant attack by US Marines, staged an epic fighting retreat back to KPA lines. In the face of the UN counter-attack, however, 1st Army abandoned Seoul, and the other armies also suffered heavily.

In the two 1951 Spring Offensives 1st Army advanced with the Chinese in the west, but the 2nd, 3rd and 5th Armies made little progress against ROK forces. In May 6th Army and 7th Army were hastily organised to defend P'yongyang and Wonsan respectively; but the expected UN offensive never materialised, and in July Lt.Gen. Nam Il, the KPA Commander and a former Soviet citizen, opened Armistice talks.

Stalemate set in, and Seoul now seemed permanently unattainable; so 1st Army (8th, 9th,

47th Divs.) transferred in December 1951 to join 2nd Army (2nd, 13th, 27th) and 3rd Army (1st, 15th, 45th) in the east. Meanwhile 4th Army (4th, 5th, 105th Armd. Divs., 26th Bde.), 5th Army (6th, 12th, 32nd), 6th Army (9th, 17th Mech., 18th, 23rd) and 7th Army (3rd, 24th, 37th, 46th Divs., 63rd Bde.) remained in reserve behind the line. The KPA was short of manpower, and war-weary; but it continued to patrol, mount local probing attacks, and infiltrate guerrillas. The July 1953 Order of Battle was:

1st Army:
8th Div. . . . 81, 82, 83 Inf.Regts.
47th Div. . . . 113, 123, 124 Inf.Regts.
2nd Army:
2nd Div. . . . 4, 6, 17 Inf.Regts.
13th Div. . . . 19, 21, 23, Inf.Regts.
27th Div. . . . 172, 173, 174 Inf.Regts.
24th Bde.
3rd Army:
1st Div. . . . 2, 3, 14, Inf.Regts.
15th Div. . . . 45, 48, 50 Inf.Regts.
37th Div. . . . 70, 71, 76 Inf.Regts.
45th Div. . . . 89, 90, 91 Inf.Regts.
4th Army:
4th Div. . . . 5, 18, 29 Inf.Regts.
5th Div. . . . 10, 11, 12 Inf.Regts.
10th Div. . . . 25, 27, 33 Inf.Regts.
5th Army:
6th Div. . . . 1, 13, 15 Inf.Regts.
12th Div. . . . 30, 31, 32 Inf.Regts.
46th Div. . . . 158, 159, 160 Inf.Regts.
20th, 22nd and 25th Bdes.
7th Army:
3rd Div. . . . 7, 8, 9 Inf.Regts.
7th Div. . . . 51, 53, 54 Inf.Regts.
9th Div. . . . 85, 86, 87 Inf.Regts.

Also 17th Div. (8, 28 and an unidentified Inf.Regt.), 21st, 23rd, 26th Bdes., 16th AA Div. (19, 20, 23, 33, 34, 36, 37 AA Regts.), four AA regts. (21, 24, 32, 38), seven tanks regts. (104, 105, 106, 107, 109, 206 and 208), two artillery regts. (29, 30) and 18 and 21 mortar regiments.

The North Korean soldier in captivity showed the same tenacity as in the field. Most PoWs, more than 100,000, were held at Koje-do (Koje Island) near Pusan, and in June 1952 they staged riots which were eventually suppressed only by the intervention of US infantry and paratroops.

Infantry of the ROK 9th Division, well equipped by the USA (mostly with M43 fatigues, in this case), assemble for an assault in 1953. The improvement in appearance since 1950 is noticeable. (US Army)

Activity at the front, however, remained low-key, although KPA units did support the June 1953 offensive by making marginal gains against ROK forces before the July Armistice.

With the Armistice, Kim Il-Sung's dreams of a united Communist Korea evaporated. North Korea was in ruins, its southern border areas shrunk, one million civilians dead, and the mighty KPA crippled by the loss of 520,000 men. But Kim has survived to this day. His army is now the fifth largest in the world—an impossible burden for such a relatively small country, comprising 520,000 soldiers, 25,000 sailors, 23,000 marines, 32,600 airmen, 40,000 Border Constabulary and almost three million Workers' Militia. These aggressive troops still line the southern border, raid South Korean offshore islands, infiltrate guerrillas, drive labyrinthine tunnels under the Armistice Line, and assault UN officials at Panmunjom.

South Korea

During the Japanese occupation Korean nationalism was brutally suppressed, and Koreans were conscripted into the Japanese forces. Politicans such as Dr Syngman Rhee operated governments-in-exile in Nationalist China and the United States, and returned to South Korea after 8 September 1945, when US troops accepted the Japanese

A variety of fatigue clothing (cf. Plates B and C) can be made out in this group photo of Col. Walter B. Richardson, CO of Camp 1 on Koje-Do, posing with ROK officers. They are (left to right) two lieutenant-colonels, a colonel, a lieutenant-colonel and a major. Note ROK collar rank insignia; and (left and centre) US-style green 'combat leader' loops worn on the shoulder straps by the battalion commander and regimental commander. Col. Richardson wears the insignia of his previous posting—the 2nd Division's 'Indian Head'—on his right shoulder. The picture was taken in August 1953. (US Army via Lee Russell)

surrender and established a temporary military government. The Korean Constabulary was formed from ex-Japanese Army veterans, and on 15 January 1946 the first battalion-size regiment was ready. On 15 August 1948 Rhee became president of an independent Republic of Korea and the 15,000-strong Constabulary became the ROK Army (*Tae-Han Min-Guk Yuk-Kun*). In May/June 1948 the six Constabulary Brigades (1st–3rd and 5th–7th: after 1948 the locally unlucky number '4' was avoided by the South, but not the North Koreans) became divisions, and the 8th and Capital Security Command were added. By 1949 the army had expanded to 60,000 men, by dint of massive United States aid, and was kept busy preventing North Korean border raids and internal subversion.

In June 1950 the 98,000-strong ROK Army under Maj. Gen. Chae Pyongdok had seven weak infantry divisions and the Capital Security Command (after 5 July the 'Capitol Division'). Each division should have had three three-battalion regiments (each of 2,938 men); a battalion comprised a heavy weapons company (with one mortar and two heavy machine gun platoons) and three rifle companies, each rifle company having three rifle platoons and a weapons platoon with a mortar and a light machine gun squad. In reality, most divisions had only two two-battalion regiments. There should have been divisional services, an anti-tank company and an artillery battalion (15 × 105 mm light howitzers in three batteries); but there were only three artillery battalions in the entire army supporting the 7th and 8th Divs. and the élite 17th Independent Regiment. The Capital Security Command was a parade unit, with the dismounted Cavalry Regt. acting as Honour Guard, but in wartime it performed well. There were no tanks, heavy mortars, mines, medium artillery or recoilless rifles; little ammunition; and only 27 M8 armoured cars in the 1st Cavalry Regiment. Only 1st, 6th, 7th and Capitol Divs. were at full strength (10,948 men), and they, together with the 8th Div. were the best units. There was also the élite Marine Corps (KMC) founded in April 1949, comprising the 1st Regt. (1st–3rd Bns.) and the independent 5th Bn., modelled on the US Marine Corps. The ROK Coastguard and Air Force were insignificant; but the National Police provided Internal Security Battalions to fight guerrillas. ROK soldiers were tough and courageous, and were often likened to the Gurkhas; but they were inexperienced, and the senior officers were too young and rarely qualified to command above battalion level.

ROK troops fought tenaciously against the initial North Korean invasion, but were no match for superior weapons, and were soon in full retreat. The 17th Regt., isolated on the Ongjin Peninsula, was evacuated by sea, abandoning its precious supporting artillery. The 1st, 2nd, 3rd, 5th, 7th and Capitol Divs. withdrew south after the fall of Seoul, and the 6th and 8th retreated in the east. Some 44,000 men, almost half the army, were trapped north of the Han River when its bridges were prematurely demolished, and their units disintegrated. On 14 July, in desperation President Rhee placed all ROK troops (now under Lt.Gen. Chung Il Kwon) under the American Gen. Walker. After an unsuccessful stand at Taejon with the US 24th Div. the shattered remnants of the ROK Army reached the northern Pusan Perimeter. There, on 24 July, the 2nd, 5th and 7th Divs. were disbanded; 8th and Capitol formed I Corps; 1st and 6th, II Corps; and 3rd guarded Army Headquarters.

These five remaining divisions clung desperately

to the northern perimeter throughout August 1950. I Corps was under intense pressure along the coast, and had to withdraw, evacuating the marooned 3rd Div. by sea; but the line held. In the west, II Corps fought alongside the US 1st Cav.Div. to hold Taegu in some of the worst fighting of the war. Meanwhile, 7th Div. was reactivated, and ROK conscripts were temporarily integrated into United States and British units as auxiliaries.

The four KMC battalions fought at Inchon and Seoul, and earned a fearsome reputation as streetfighters. I Corps (3rd and Capitol Divs., KMAG) sped from Pusan up the east coast; II Corps (6th, 7th, 8th) pushed through the central mountains; and 1st Div. joined US I Corps at Seoul. By 10 October I Corps had reached Wonsan *en route* for Hŭngnam. III Corps (formed 8 October) remained in South Korea on security duties with 11th Division (also formed in October) and 5th Division. In that same month the 1st Anti-Guerrilla Group (1st–3rd, 5th–7th Bns.) was formed. On 19 October 1st Div. took P'yongyang, and joined II Corps further north. On 24 October 7th Regt. (6th Div.) reached the Yalu River; but the next day this division was smashed by an overwhelming Chinese attack, and only the arrival of 7th Div. prevented the total collapse of II Corps and stabilised the line.

By 24 November Capitol Div. had reached Chongjin, 60 miles from the Soviet border; but on the next day the Chinese, taking advantage of the low firepower of ROK divisions and the primitive fear the Chinese inspired among Koreans, attacked II Corps again. The corps cracked, necessitating a general 8th Army retreat to the 38th Parallel. Meanwhile the exposed Capitol and 3rd Divs. fell back to Songjin and Hŭngnam respectively, and were evacuated to South Korea.

By mid-December 1950 1st Div. (US I Corps) was manning the line in the west; in the centre, III Corps (2nd Div. reformed 7th November, 5th and 11th Divs.); then the weakened II Corps (6th, 7th, 8th Divs.); and on the coast I Corps (9th Div., formed 25 October; 3rd, Capitol Divs.). When the 1951 New Year offensive struck, 6th Div. was promptly attached to US IX Corps, and II Corps was disbanded. On 2 January 2nd, 5th and 8th Divs. joined US X Corps, which took over most of the vulnerable central sector from III Corps (now with 7th and 11th Divs.). In the UN retreat 2nd and

The commander of the US 1st Marine Division, Maj.Gen. Oliver P. Smith (left, in the Marines' characteristic HBT 'utilities' and camouflaged helmet cover), talks to US X Corps commander Maj.Gen. Edward M. Almond (right, in M43 fatigues). Photographed at Seoul in September 1950, Smith would within two months be leading the famous fighting retreat of his division from Chosin Reservoir. Just visible at far right is 1st Marine Air Wing commander Maj.Gen. Field Harris, whose Corsair squadrons provided valuable support. (USMC)

9th Divs. virtually distintegrated, and Communist troops poured through gaps in ROK lines. In the January UN counter-offensive III Corps had difficulty keeping up; and, on 11 February north of Hoengsan, the 3rd (with 1st KMC Regt. attached), 5th and 8th Divs. took the brunt of a heavy Chinese attack, which destroyed the 8th Div. (it later reformed). However, by mid-April 1951 I and III Corps were safely in position on 'Line Utah' just inside North Korea.

In the 1951 First Spring Offensive the Chinese concentrated their attack on the 1st and 6th Divs. in the west, and both formations fell back; but a determined stand by 5th KMC Bn. on the Kimpo Peninsula prevented an attack on Seoul. Gen. Van Fleet moved 2nd Div. to join the 6th in US IX Corps, leaving US X Corps with 5th and 7th Divs. In the Second Spring Offensive these last two divisions and III Corps all collapsed, and even I Corps retreated; but by 20 May the line had stabilised. Now III Corps was disbanded, leaving only I Corps (3rd, 11th, Capitol Divs.) in the line. I Corps subsequently attacked, together with 5th, 7th, 8th and 9th Divs., now all in US X Corps.

Despite catastrophic setbacks the ROK Army, now under Maj.Gen. Yi Chongchan, still fielded ten divisions; and in August 1951 357,430 South Koreans, the largest UNC contingent, were under arms.

The ROK Army took advantage of the stalemate period to build up its forces. Four 155 mm and six 105 mm Artillery Battalions, authorised in September 1951, ensured that by mid-1952 ROK divisions at last had their own organic artillery. There were also ten Field Artillery Groups (1st–3rd, 5th–11th), each with two 105 mm battalions; and 11 Independent Field Artillery Bns. (88th–93rd, 95th 99th. Other units included eight Tank Companies (51st–53rd, 55th–59th); 13 Security Bns. (1st–3rd, 5th–13th, 15th) on anti-guerrilla duties; five Security Guard Bns. (31st–33rd, 35th, 36th) guarding PoW camps; and Korean Service Corps Regts. (each with four battalions) on labouring duties with UN units. On 1 May 1952 the order of battle at the front was: US I Corps (1st Div.); US IX Corps (2nd, 9th); a re-formed II Corps (3rd, 6th, Capitol); US X Corps (7th, 8th) and I Corps (5th, 11th).

The revitalised army, now under Lt.Gen. Paik Sun Yup, performed very effectively in the 1952 'Outpost' battles, and could now be trusted with three-quarters of the line. More units were raised: 12th and 15th Divs., 53rd and 55th–59th Independent Regts. (November 1952); 20th and 21st Divs. (February 1953); 22nd and 25th Divs. (April 1953); and 26th and 27th Divs. (June 1953). In the Chinese attacks of June 1953 II Corps fell back but held, although 5th Div. had to be rescued. Nevertheless, 14 ROK divisions faced the final assault in July: 1st Div. (US I Corps); 2nd, 9th, Capitol (US IX Corps); 3rd, 5th, 6th, 8th, 11th (II Corps); 7th, 12th, 20th (US X Corps); 15th and 21st (I Corps). The concentrated pressure on II Corps smashed the redoubtable Capitol Div., and the Corps fell back; but subsequently counter-attacked, and reached a viable defence line before the Armistice.

In its comparatively short life the ROK Army had withstood the most punishing ordeal imaginable; had lost about 47,000 killed; and had emerged as the determined guarantor of the independence of the South Korean people.

The ROK Army order of battle, September 1950–July 1953, was:

1st Div. . . . 11th, 12th, 15th Regts.
2nd Div. . . . 17th, 31st, 32nd Regts.
3rd Div. . . . 22nd, 23rd, 26th, (later 18th, 22nd, 23rd Regts.)
5th Div. . . . 27th, 35th, 36th Regts.
6th Div. . . . 2nd, 7th, 19th, Regts.
7th Div. . . . 3rd, 5th, 8th Regts.
8th Div. . . . 10th, 16th, 21st Regts.
9th Div. . . . 28th, 29th, 30th Regts.
Capitol Div. . . . 1st, 17th, 18th, (later 1st Cav., 26th Regts.)
11th Div. . . . 9th, 13th, 20th Regts.
12th Div. . . . 37th, 51st, 52nd Regts.
15th Div. . . . 38th, 39th, 50th Regts.
20th Div. . . . 60th, 61st, 62nd Regts.
21st Div. . . . 63rd, 65th, 66th Regts.
22nd Div. . . . 67th, 68th, 69th Regts.
25th Div. . . . 70th, 71st, 72nd Regts.
26th Div. . . . 73rd, 75th, 76th Regts.
27th Div. . . . 77th, 78th, 79th Regts.

United States of America

After 1945 the United States decided to rely on the United States Air Force to deter any future aggressor with its nuclear capability. There thus seemed to be no necessity for a large standing army, and the bulk of the US Army was hastily demobilised. By mid-1950 it had shrunk to 591,487 men, seven per cent of its peak wartime strength, with what some have judged to be a disastrous effect

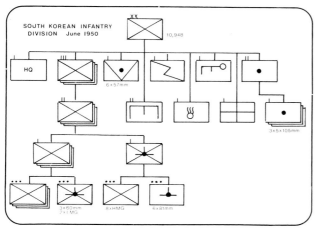

SOUTH KOREAN INFANTRY DIVISION June 1950

on unit efficiency and morale. There were only ten combat divisions—1st, 2nd, 3rd, 7th, 24th and 25th Infantry, 1st Cavalry (Dismounted), 2nd Armoured, 11th and 82nd Airborne—plus the 1st and 2nd US Marine Corps Divisions[1]. Occupation duty in Germany and Japan proved the biggest drain on resources, and only one division, the 1st Infantry in Germany, was maintained at full strength.

In South Korea, too, United States airpower was the main defence against potential North Korean aggression, and after June 1949 the only US forces were the 500-strong Korean Military Advisory Group (KMAG) training the fledgling ROK Army. Meanwhile, the United States Government ignored rumours of an imminent North Korean invasion with a complacency that ultimately proved disastrous.

At any one time seven United States divisions—Infantry, Cavalry and Marine Corps—served in Korea, all in the infantry rôle. This commitment, while modest by World War II standards, was a major burden on the diminished US Army. Each division contained three infantry regiments (each with three battalions); and an artillery regiment with three 105 mm battalions and one heavy 155 mm battalion, each with three batteries. (The strength of the US artillery was to prove decisive.) There were also a combat engineer battalion, reconnaissance troops, and services; and later a tank, a tank-destroyer and an anti-aircraft battalion were added. Apart from the three rifle battalions (each with one heavy weapons and three rifle companies) a US infantry regiment also fielded a tank company with 22 tanks. A rifle company comprised one weapons and three rifle platoons; a rifle platoon, one weapons squad and three rifle squads, each with nine men.

All divisions (except the Marines) were 30 per cent under strength. All regiments (except the Negro 24th Infantry) had only two battalions: artillery battalions had only two batteries, and most infantry battalions were a rifle company short, although from August 1950 all regiments in Korea received a third battalion. Many tanks were obsolescent, or too light to meet the T-34/85 on equal terms. Nevertheless, these divisions did boast

Pusan, January 1951: the US Army's 51st Signals Bn. Personnel Section, in a soldier's typical snapshot. The sergeant at far left wears on his HBT fatigues the new chevrons officially introduced the following month; the miniature 'combat chevrons' are worn by the young sergeant in the pile winter cap, right centre. (Shelby Stanton)

an awesome firepower, especially in artillery, which outclassed comparable enemy units[1].

For special missions a regiment could become a 'regimental combat team (equivalent to a British 'brigade group') by attaching a divisional 105 mm artillery battalion, a signals detachment, and engineer and medical companies. At least 12 infantry regiments (7th, 15th, 19th, 21st, 23rd, 24th, 31st, 32nd, 34th, 35th, 65th, 160th) operated at some time as RCTs, as well as the independent 5th and 29th, and the famous 187th Airborne (detached from 11th Airborne Division). Other élite units were the 1st–5th and 8th Ranger Infantry Companies (Airborne), each with five officers and 107 men, including the all-black 2nd Co., in Korea from October 1950 to August 1951; and the mixed American–British–Korean 'United Nations Partisan Infantry Korea' (UNPIK). These units all operated clandestinely behind enemy lines and on the offshore islands.

The scattered KMAG advisers retreated helplessly with the ROK divisions before the North Korean advance, an advance which immediate USAF air strikes were unable to halt. United States Army intervention was necessary, and four of the five divisions of Lt.Gen. Walton H. Walker's 8th Army (7th, 24th, 25th Infantry, 1st Cavalry), then

[1]For an account of the USMC's condition at this time see Elite 2, *The US Marine Corps since 1945*.

[1]For a detailed account of UN tank operations in Korea, see Vanguard 27, *Armour of the Korean War*.

Fine study of a US Army rifle squad leader in autumn 1950: Cpl. Carroll Vogles of the 35th RCT, based on the 35th Infantry from 25th Division. No unit or rank insignia are worn in the field. He carries the M1 rifle, and a triple-pocket grenade pouch (left) and first aid pouch are attached to his rifle belt. The extra bandoliers are typical enough—but one suspects that the grenades, rather precariously attached by slipping their spoons into pockets, were the photographer's idea . . . in combat they would be rather more securely attached to the equipment. (US Army via Shelby Stanton)

on occupation duty in Japan, were put on alert. On 1 July 1950 'Task Force Smith'—two rifle companies from 21st Inf.Regt. (24th Div.) reinforced by 105 mm howitzer, mortar, bazooka and recoilless rifle teams—raced to the front, and managed to delay the enemy advance on Osan before retreating to meet the rest of the division. The 24th made a heroic stand at Taejon, but abandoned the town on 20 July, having lost their commander, Maj.Gen. Dean. They had bought time for the safe arrival of the 25th Infantry and 1st Cavalry Divs., and the 29th RCT from Okinawa. On 13 July Gen. Walker established 'EUSAK' (Eighth United States Army in Korea) within the Pusan perimeter, where he also commanded five ROK divisions. All forces in Korea came under Gen. MacArthur, since 7 July the Supreme Commander of United Nations Command (UNC).

By the end of July the perimeter line had stabilised along the Naktong River, to be defended at all costs. In August reinforcements arrived in the form of divisional tank battalions, the 5th RCT from Hawaii, the 2nd Inf.Div. and 1st Provisional Marine Bde. (built around 5th Marine Regt.) from the USA, and the 27th British Brigade. South Korean conscripts, designated 'Katusas' (Koreans attached to the US Army), were integrated into the US Army and unofficially into USMC units, with 100 per company, a total of between 1,000 and 3,000 per division. Wearing US uniforms (but rarely attaining NCO rank) these enthusiastic, fearless, but virtually untrained Koreans provided a vital stopgap in manpower. Walker's nine divisions and two brigades were insufficient for a continuous defensive line; but he deployed them so skilfully in anticipation of enemy attacks that he was able to win the fierce six-week 'Perimeter Battles', and by mid-September he was ready to counter-attack.

On 15 September, United States X Corps (activated in Japan on 26 August) stormed ashore at Inchon with 1st Marine Div. (the expanded Provisional Bde.), 7th Inf.Div. (including ROK 17th Regt. and 8,000 Katusas), 5th RCT and, later, 187 ARCT. On 28 September Seoul was recaptured after fierce fighting. Meanwhile, on 16 September, EUSAK forces broke out of the Pusan perimeter. ROK forces thrust northwards, US IX Corps (activated on 23 September with 2nd and 25th Divs.) attacked westwards, and US I Corps (activated 13 September with 1st Cav., 24th Inf. and 1st ROK Divs. and 27th Bde.) pushed north-westwards, linking up with X Corps on 26 September. On 1 October Walker began the advance into North Korea. I Corps (later joined by IX Corps) attacked along the west coast, taking P'yongyang on the 19th, while the ROKs advanced in the east, joined by X Corps (now with 3rd Inf.Div. from the USA), which landed at Wonsan on 26 October. However, this triumphant progress ground to a halt in November with the intervention of the Chinese.

The furthest UN penetration northwards was by the 17th Regt., which reached the Chinese–North Korean border at Hyesanjin. On 24 November MacArthur ordered the final push to the Yalu River frontier; but after 24 hours' steady advance a powerful Chinese counter-attack ruptured the line in the central sector, forcing I and IX Corps to retreat southwards to avoid encirclement. By 15 December they and three ROK Corps, now out of reach of the Chinese advance, had established a defensive line on the 38th Parallel. Meanwhile, on 27 November, X Corps, marooned in north-eastern Korea, began an epic fighting retreat to Hŭngnam,

December 1951—a US Marine squad return from patrol. They wear their helmets stuffed down over pile caps and—in the case of the foreground man, carrying the 'folded' M20 3.5 in. rocket launcher—over the hood of the parka. (The hood was supposed to accommodate the helmet, but was seldom worn that way.) The parka is identified as the light tan-coloured World War II model by the skirt pockets: the M1951 model, issued towards the end of the war, had only the slanting pockets on the ribs. (USMC)

where 193 UN ships, under a massive air umbrella, successfully evacuated them. By Christmas Day 105,000 troops had embarked for Pusan in the biggest sea evacuation in American history. Then, on 23 December, Gen. Walker was killed in a traffic accident, to be replaced as EUSAK Commander on the 26th by Lt.Gen. Matthew B. Ridgway.

Ridgway had 365,000 troops—from west to east, US I Corps (25th, 3rd Inf., 1st ROK Divs.); IX Corps (1st Cav., 1st Marine, 24th Inf., 6th ROK Divs.); three ROK Corps; and X Corps (2nd, 7th Inf., 2nd, 5th, 8th ROK) in reserve. The Chinese New Year offensive brought X Corps into the central sector, and forced I and IX Corps to abandon Seoul on 4 January 1951. However, by 15 January the offensive had run out of steam, and on the 25th EUSAK, now just south of Osan, counter-attacked strongly northwards against determined Chinese opposition. Meanwhile the 1st Marine Div. fought the North Korean 10th Div., cut off deep in South Korea, before joining the IX Corps advance in February. On 14 March I Corps recaptured Seoul, and by mid-April Ridgway's forces had reached 'Line Utah', just inside North Korea. On 11 April, after a dramatic disagreement over the issue of widening the scope of operations against China, President Truman replaced the legendary Gen. MacArthur with Gen. Ridgway, who in turn passed EUSAK command to Lt.Gen. James Van Fleet.

In the First Spring Offensive I and IX Corps—defending the approaches to Seoul—were attacked, but held firm. By 29 April the offensive was spent, and Van Fleet pushed forward gingerly with armoured patrols. Order of battle was now I Corps (1st Cav., 3rd and 25th Inf.Divs.), IX Corps (7th and 24th Inf., 2nd and 6th ROK Divs., 187th ARCT), and X Corps (1st Marine, 2nd Inf., 5th and 7th ROK Divs.). The Second Spring Offensive on 16 May smashed ROK divisions in X Corps, but other units plugged the gap as the Corps fell back, and attacks on I and IX Corps were similarly contained. Now Van Fleet counter-attacked strongly; and on 21 May advanced against light resistance to 'Line Wyoming' back in North Korea, which he fortified with trenches, wire, mines and artillery. The truce talks reduced activity to local level, but X Corps fought successfully to improve its position. Meanwhile, on 6 April the 65th (Puerto

Col. Frederick B. Alexander, CO of the 21st Infantry, 24th Division, early 1953. Note combat boots fitted with zippers; and regimental crest worn on 'combat leader's' green shoulder strap loop, above the divisional shoulder sleeve insignia. (US Army)

Rico) Inf.Regt. replaced the 30th in 3rd Div.; and on 1 August (the day Van Fleet was promoted full general) the 14th Inf. joined 25th Div., replacing the black 24th Regt., which was disbanded.

Now stalemate set in, as Ridgway ordered EUSAK to stop advancing but actively to defend its forward positions in North Korea. In December 1951 the 1st Cav.Div. was replaced in I Corps by 45th (Oklahoma) Div., one of four National Guard divisions called into Federal service in August 1950. In late January 1952 a sister division, the 40th (California), replaced the veteran 24th Div. in IX Corps. Throughout January massive air and artillery strikes rained down on Chinese positions, but thereafter activity was light, despite a major but unsuccessful enemy offensive in May against I Corps. On 12 May the veteran World War II commander Gen. Mark Clark replaced Ridgway as UNC Commander. In June the 187th ARCT was used to crush the revolt on Koje Island off Pusan.

July 1952 saw the 'Battle of the Outposts'. In October 2nd Div. (I Corps) repelled a strong Chinese attack, while IX Corps advanced gradually into the 'Iron Triangle', inflicting huge casualties. By January 1953 Van Fleet had 768,000 troops disposed (from west to east) in I Corps (2nd, 7th, later 25th, Inf.; 1st Marine; 1st, 2nd, 15th ROK Divs.); IX Corps (3rd Inf.; 9th ROK, ROK Capitol); ROK II Corps; X Corps (40th, 45th Inf.; 7th 12th, 20th ROK); and ROK I Corps. On 11 February 1953 Van Fleet retired after nearly two years as EUSAK Commander, and was replaced by Lt.Gen. (from 23 June, Gen.) Maxwell D. Taylor. In March and May I Corps withstood heavy enemy attacks, and were reinforced in June by 187th ARCT and 34th RCT (24th Div.) from Japan. On 10 June a powerful Chinese offensive against ROK II Corps forced the neighbouring X Corps back three miles. Then, on 13 July, IX Corps contained with difficulty the last major Chinese penetration before the Armistice of 27 July.

The United States emerged from the Korean War as undeniably the principal Western power in succession to Great Britain and France, accepting world-wide obligations, especially in the containment of Communism. The 1945 concept of total war, waged by aircraft carrying atomic weapons, gave way to the concept of limited war, requiring a standing army which must never again decline to the dangerously low levels of the late 1940s. Tactically, the infantry reasserted its traditional position as the key arm, which it had apparently lost

to armour. The importance of artillery firepower was re-emphasised; Ranger and Airborne units had been so successful that their training methods were extended to all infantry officers; and the growth of Army (especially helicopter) aviation presaged the birth of the 'airmobile' concept.

The United States divisional order of battle in Korea was:

2nd Inf.Div. . . . 9th, 23rd, 38th Inf.Regts.; 12th*, 15th, 37th, 38th Arty.Bns.; 72nd Tk.Bn.; 2nd Eng.Bn.; 82nd AA Bn.

3rd Inf.Div. . . . 7th, 15th, 30th (replaced by 65th Puerto Rico) Inf.Regts.; 9th*, 10th, 39th, 58th Arty.Bns.; 64th Tk.Bn.; 10th Eng.Bn.; 3rd AA Bn.

7th Inf.Div. . . . 17th, 31st, 32nd Inf.Regts.; 31st*, 48th, 49th, 57th Arty.Bns.; 73rd Tk.Bn.; 13th Eng.Bn.; 15th AA Bn.

24th Inf.Div. . . . 19th, 21st, 34th Inf.Regts.; 11th*, 13th, 52nd, 63rd Arty.Bns.; 70th Tk.Bn.; 3rd Eng.Bn.; 26th AA Bn.

25th Inf.Div. . . . 24th (replaced by 14th), 27th, 35th Inf.Regts.; 8th, 64th, 69th, 90th* Arty.Bns.; 89th Tk.Bn.; 65th Eng.Bn.; 21st AA Bn.

40th Inf.Div. . . . 160th, 223rd, 224th Inf.Regts.; 143rd, 625th, 980th, 981st* Arty.Bns.; 140th Tk.Bn.; 578th Eng.Bn.; 140th AA Bn.

45th Inf.Div. . . . 179th, 180th, 279th Inf.Regts.; 158th, 160th, 171st, 189th* Arty.Bns.; 245th Tk.Bn.; 120th Eng.Bn.; 145th AA Bn.

1st Cav.Div. . . . 5th, 7th, 8th Cav.Regts.; 61st, 77th 82nd*, 99th, Arty.Bns.; 6th Tk.Bn.; 8th Eng.Bn.; 29th AA Bn.

1st Mar.Div. . . . 1st, 5th, 7th Mar.Regts.; 1st, 2nd, 3rd, 4th Bns.; 11th Arty.Regt.; 1st Tk.Bn.; 1st Eng.Bn.; 1st Amph.Bn.

(*denotes 155 mm artillery battalion)

British Commonwealth

After 1945 the British Army began to demobilise; but the British government recognised the necessity of a credible peacetime army, and so conscription (in 1948 renamed 'National Service') was retained for men aged 18–20. Britain had traditional Imperial commitments to which were now added new international obligations—occupation forces

Field Marshal Lord Alexander of Tunis, the British Defence Minister, inspects an Honor Guard from the US 3rd Infantry Division wearing HBT fatigues much dressed up for the occasion with the division's blue and white insignia, matching scarves, polished and badged helmet liners, and other typical parade features. (Imperial War Museum)

Bugle-Major Martin, Durham Light Infantry, 'warms up' his buglers for a fanfare. They wear the regimental cap badge on the midnight blue beret which was (and remains) the general issue for British troops, though now replaced in the LI by dark green. The field jacket and trousers are the type later designated M58 combat dress; note Commonwealth Division shield and regimental title on right shoulders. The bugle-major's four chevrons are worn on the upper, rather than the lower sleeve as was regulation. (The Light Infantry)

in Germany and Japan, and NATO requirements for troops to defend Western Europe. Similarly, in Canada, Australia and New Zealand membership of Western military alliances was accepted as essential to the security of national independence.

The North Korean invasion, so soon after the Communist victory in China, was seen as a further step towards Communist world domination. Immediately 17 ships and 7,000 men of the Royal, Royal Australian and Royal New Zealand Navies were sent to Korea. They were followed on 29 June by 77 (Fighter) Sqn. RAAF, flying Mustangs, and subsequently by 30 (Transport) Unit RAAF, 426 (Transport) Sqn. RCAF, and, in November, the Mustangs of 2 Sqn. SAAF, the 'Flying Cheetahs'. In August 27th Infantry Brigade, the United Kingdom Strategic Reserve then stationed with 40th Div. in Hong Kong, was earmarked for Korea.

A British or Commonwealth infantry brigade (equivalent to a US regiment) consisted of headquarters, services, and three rifle battalions each 909 men strong. A rifle battalion had an HQ company (with signals and administration platoons); a support company (mortar, machine gun, anti-tank and assault pioneer platoons); and four

rifle companies (A-D) each with three rifle platoons (1st–9th within the company). A platoon had three rifle sections, each with a corporal and eight men. In peacetime most battalions had only three rifle companies, and so for Korea a fourth was raised from neighbouring battalions. During this period there was a high incidence of 'cross posting' to bring units up to strength for tours in Korea. The troops were a mixture of long-service regulars, wartime reservists recalled to the colours, and national service conscripts. Some of the latter were given the option of volunteering, but this was not general.

On 28 August 1950 27th Bde. (really a 'brigade group', as it operated with organic supporting arms) disembarked at Pusan with only two battalions—1st Argyll and Sutherland Highlanders and 1st Middlesex Regt.—and immediately manned the western perimeter, supported by two US artillery batteries and some US tanks. On 18 September they broke out, and advanced north-westwards with US 24th Div., meeting fierce enemy opposition (against which Maj. Muir of the Argylls earned a posthumous Victoria Cross). On 1 October the brigade was renamed 27th Commonwealth Inf.Bde., being brought up to strength by the arrival of 3rd Bn., Royal Australian Regt., a formidable all-regular unit. During the rapid advance up the west coast the Australians killed 270 North Koreans in a bayonet charge north of P'yongyang. On 30 October the brigade had reached Chongju, 40 miles from the Manchurian border, when the Chinese intervention forced a withdrawal to Sinanju; here the brigade beat off a determined Chinese attack. Meanwhile, the 250-strong 41st (Independent) Commando, Royal Marines, formed in Japan in September 1950 for Korean service, mounted two raids against the east coast in early October, and in November joined US 1st Marine Div. (X Corps) isolated in NE Korea.

Following the Chinese attack of 25 November 27th Bde., now in US IX Corps reserve, supported the general retreat south, meeting the British 29th Independent Brigade Group, which had disembarked at Pusan on 3 November and was now advancing north. On 14 December 27th Bde., now on the 38th Parallel defence line, was joined by 60th (Parachute) Indian Field Ambulance, India's only but distinguished contribution to the war-effort. The 29th Brigade—which as well as three infantry battalions fielded tank[1], artillery and engineer units—had been fighting North Korean guerrillas near Seoul before moving up to P'yongyang, only to retreat again to the 38th Parallel in mid-December. Meanwhile, 41 Commando performed a magnificent fighting withdrawal with US 1st Marine Div. from the Chosin Reservoir to Hŭngnam for evacuation to South Korea.

In December 1950 all ground, sea and air forces became the British Commonwealth Forces in Korea (BCFK), HQ Japan, under Lt.Gen. Sir Horace Robertson, the first of three Australians to hold the command. The 27th Bde. (US IX Corps) retreated in good order before the 1951 New Year offensive; 29th Bde. (US I Corps), covering Seoul, fought fiercely at Chungghung Dong, and crossed the Han River after suffering heavy casualties. By mid-January the two brigades were entrenched well south of Seoul. Then the slow UN winter counter-offensive northwards began. 27th Brigade at last received its own organic artillery battalion—16th Field Regt., Royal New Zealand Artillery; and on 18 February 2nd Bn., Princess Patricia's Canadian Light Infantry became its fourth infantry battalion. By 19 April both brigades had halted well north of Seoul, 29th Bde. on the Imjin River.

The First Spring Offensive struck 29th Bde. with massive force and they fell back, leaving 1st Gloucesters cut off on Point 235 ('Gloucester Hill') to conduct a heroic last stand which bought time for other units, and ultimately blunted the offensive. After two and a half days just 39 Gloucesters reached UN lines; Lt.Col. Carne, the battalion commander, and Lt. Curtis were both awarded the Victoria Cross. The battle of the Imjin River was the Commonwealth's finest hour in Korea. 27th Bde. fought its way southwards, and on 26 April 1951 became 28th Commonwealth Bde. (the only brigade to be 'relieved'). In early May, 25th Canadian Infantry Brigade Group arrived with three infantry battalions (including 2nd PPCLI, transferred from 28th Bde.), an artillery regiment, a field ambulance (both battalion equivalents), and tank and engineer squadrons. In the May UN counter-offensive 25th Bde. (US I Corps), 28th and 29th Bdes. (US IX Corps) all advanced to a new

Two British soldiers of the DLI pose with a 'Katcom' before going out on patrol, 1952–53. They wear cap comforters—knit caps, rolled from a tube of wool; US M1951 (left) and M1952 'flak jackets'; and carry Stens and grenades. (The Light Infantry)

defensive line inside North Korea. There, on 28 July 1951, the 1st Commonwealth Division was formed from the existing three infantry brigades, a tank regiment and squadron, three artillery regiments and two batteries, an engineer regiment and two squadrons, and three field ambulances. The division defended Seoul under US I Corps; and in October advanced northwards in Operation 'Commando', during which 1st KOSB (28th Bde.) suffered heavily in Chinese counter-attacks. It was during this battle that Pte. Speakman won his VC.

The stalemate period allowed the division's British, Canadian, Australian, New Zealand and Indian units to reach a level of efficient co-operation, spiced with friendly rivalry, which still stands as a model for multi-national military formations. The intense winter cold of 1951–2 brought welfare problems not encountered since the Crimean War, but military activity was restricted to patrols and raids. In late May 1952 two companies served on Koje-do PoW Camp as prison guards. Meanwhile 41 Cdo. RM, after coastal

[1]For detailed accounts of British tank operations, see Vanguards 22, *The Centurion Tank in Battle*, and 27, *Armour of the Korean War*.

raiding throughout 1951, left Korea, and was disbanded at Plymouth in February 1952.

Static warfare continued throughout the winter of 1952–3, but improved Chinese defensive fire made local raiding increasingly unattractive. The front was quiet, although in late October divisional artillery did support the neighbouring 1st US Marine Div. when they came under attack. 1,000 ROK conscripts were integrated as 'Katcoms' ('Koreans Attached Commonwealth Division'), with two Katcoms per infantry section. They wore the relevant unit uniform; could be promoted to NCO rank; and were liked and respected. During November 1952 1st Black Watch repelled a determined Chinese attack against the hill known as 'The Hook'. The division spent two months in reserve from February 1953; and in late May the 1st Duke of Wellington's Regt., supported by artillery and the Centurions of 1st RTR, again defended

A Scottish soldier serving in Korea being fitted with the second type of winter warfare clothing issued in response to the sufferings of British troops during the appallingly cold winter of 1950. (Imperial War Museum)

The Hook in the last sizeable Commonwealth engagement of the war—although infantry and artillery did help the US Marines in the last desperate fighting before the Armistice.

Commonwealth losses, at 1,263 dead of whom 686 were British, were considered moderate; and the division stayed in South Korea until 1956, when it was replaced by a 2,000-strong Contingent, which was steadily reduced over the years which followed. The unique experiment of the multi-national division, although successful, is unlikely ever to be repeated in the entirely different strategic conditions which now face the separate nations of the Old Commonwealth.

The order of battle of Commonwealth ground forces (excluding 41 Cdo. Royal Marines) follows below. Diagonal strokes represent successive deployments: e.g. the initial infantry units of 29th Bde. were 1st Bn., Royal Northumberland Fusiliers; 1st Bn., The Gloucestershire Regt.; and 1st Bn., Royal Ulster Rifles. (In the lists below, titles have been greatly abbreviated.) Canadian and British units rotated (very approximately) every 12 months; India and New Zealand rotated personnel occasionally; Australia did both.

27th/28th Commonwealth Infantry Brigade
1st Middx./1st KSLI/1st DLI/1st Warwicks
1st Argylls/1st KOSB/1st R. Fusiliers/1st Essex
3rd R. Australians/1st R. Australians/2nd R. Australians
2nd PPCLI
16th Fd.Regt. RNZA
60th Indian (Para) Fd.Amb.

29th British Infantry Brigade Group
1st Northumberlands/1st Leicesters/1st Black Watch/1st R. Scots
1st Gloucesters/1st Welch/1st Dk of Wellington's
1st Ulsters/1st Norfolks/1st Liverpool
'C' Sqn. 7th Royal Tank Regt.
8th Irish Hussars/5th Inniskillings/1st RTR/5th RTR
45th/14th/20th Fd.Regt. RA
170th/120th Lt. Battery RA (Mortars)/61st Lt. Regt. RA
11th/42nd Lt. AA Bn. RA
55th & 122nd Fd.SqnRE, 64th Fd.Pk.Sqn.RE/28th Fd.Eng.Regt.RE
26th Fd.Amb.

25th Canadian Infantry Brigade Group
2nd/1st/3rd R. Canadians
2nd/1st/3rd R.22ᵉ Regt.
2nd/1st/3rd PPCLI
'C'/'B'/'A' Sqn. Lord Strathcona's Horse
2nd/1st R.Can. Horse Arty./81st Fd.Regt. RCA
23rd Fd.Sqn. RCE/28th Fd.Eng.Regt. RE
57th Indep.Fd.Sqn. RCE
25th/37th/38th Can.Fd.Amb.
25th Can.Fd. Dressing Stat.

1st Comm. Div. Sigs. Regt.
1903rd Indep.AOP Flight

Other United Nations Contingents

Three days after the North Korean invasion the United Nations called on all member states to help South Korea. Ten countries, besides the Commonwealth, sent armed units, and four sent medical teams. The soldiers, all volunteers, were idealists, adventurers, or regulars hoping for accelerated promotion through recent combat experience. In all cases (except the Philippines) special units were raised and they, or their personnel, were regularly rotated.

First came the **Philippines**. The army, re-organised in early 1950 into ten US-style 'battalion combat teams' to fight the Huk Communists, sent the experienced 10th BCT (Motorised) and a Medium Tank Company. With 1,367 men in three rifle companies, light tank and reconnaissance (jeep) companies, a self-propelled artillery battery and supporting services, the unit could operate independently. Troops wore uniforms identical to the US Army with the Philippine cap badge, and US rank insignia including pre-1948 chevrons. They disembarked at Pusan on 20 September 1950; and operated with US 25th Div. on anti-guerrilla duties—their speciality. From January 1951 the unit served with US 3rd Div., and in April its tanks tried unsuccessfully to relieve the Gloucesters at the Imjin River. The 20th BCT took over in September 1951, serving from April 1952 with US 45th Div.; in June 1952 it was relieved by 19th BCT ('Blood-

An MP of the Canadian Provost Corps, 25th Bde., 1st Commonwealth Division. Note sleeve insignia worn on two brassards: on his left arm the divisional sign, on his right the red 'Canada' shield with a gold-yellow maple leaf and wreath, both under regimental titles. (Public Archives Canada)

hounds'); in April 1953 by 14th BCT ('Avengers'), and finally, in April 1954, by 2nd BCT.

After World War II **Turkey** was driven by fear of its Soviet neighbour into the Western camp. Although at peace since 1923, Turkish troops were generally considered the best of the smaller UN contingents; they fought well, especially in close combat; were steadfast in defence, and resolute as PoWs; and were well led. The 1st Turkish Brigade—with 241st Inf.Regt. (three battalions), an artillery battalion, signals platoon, and engineer, transport, medical and ordnance companies—disembarked at Pusan 5,455 strong, on 18–20 October 1950, and advanced with 25th US Div. into North Korea. They met the Chinese intervention head on, fighting desperately but being beaten back at Sinnimini with heavy losses. They fought doggedly near Osan in February 1951, and on 15 May foiled another direct Chinese assault. On 1 September 1951 2nd Bde. took over; on 30 July 1952, 3rd Bde.; and on 4 September 1953, 4th Bde.; which left Korea in May 1954.

A captain of the French *Bataillon de Corée* wearing the black beret and badge illustrated in Plate F1—note large eyelets in beret. French and American decorations are worn on US fatigues, including the battalion's lanyard for four collective citations, in the colours—yellow flecked with green—of the *Médaille Militaire* ribbon. Three gold bars pinned to the chest indicate his rank. (E.C.P. Armées)

Thailand sent the 'Royal Thai Forces in Korea'—air and naval forces and the 21st Inf.Regt., formed 22 September 1950 with HQ and 1st Bn. only. It reached Korea on 22 October, and advanced with the US 187th ARCT to P'yongyang. In January 1951 the unit retreated with the British 29th Bde. under Chinese pressure; and, with 1st US Cav.Div., fought guerrillas and faced the Spring Offensives. In December 1951 they patrolled with US 9th Inf. (2nd Div.), fighting gallantly at Pork Chop Hill. The regiment returned home on 31 March 1955, leaving a company-sized contingent which remained until 1972, by which time 19,000 Thais had served tours in Korea; wartime service cost them 125 dead. The 21st Regt. is now HM Queen Sirikit's Guard Unit.

In spite of the heavy burden of her war in Indochina **France** sent the UN French Forces under Lt.Gen. (temporary Lt.Col!) Monclar[1], commanding an HQ and the French Battalion (Bataillon Français), with HQ company (including an élite assault pioneer platoon), support company and three rifle companies (1st–3rd), each with one support and three rifle platoons. They disembarked at Pusan on 29 November 1950, and joined the 23rd RCT (2nd US Division). The battalion distinguished itself in a bayonet charge at Wonju on 10 January 1951, and in an epic defence of Chip'yong-ni village from 13 to 17 February, which turned the Chinese offensive. At Putchaetul (17 May) the pioneers fought to the death. Heartbreak Ridge was captured in October 1951, and Arrow Head Hill held in October 1952, but again at the cost of the pioneers. On 22 October 1953 the French set sail for the Indochina War, leaving 261 dead in Korea.

Netherlands naval forces reached Korea in July 1950; but the Dutch Army, seriously depleted after their recent war in Indonesia, could offer only an understrength infantry battalion from the recently formed Regiment Van Heutsz. The 636-strong unit—with headquarters, HQ company, one support and two rifle companies and some nurses, all under Major den Ouden—reached Pusan on 23 November 1950, and joined US 38th Inf. (US 2nd Div.) in a particularly successful partnership. On 12 February 1951 the headquarters and HQ Co. were overrun by Chinese disguised as ROK troops, and den Ouden was killed. In May a third rifle company arrived, and in April to July 1952 it helped quell the PoW revolt on Koje-do. In September 1954 the battalion left Korea, having lost 120 dead.

Exhausted after a long civil war **Greece** nevertheless sent a reinforced battalion formed from volunteers from the Greek Army's 1st, 8th and 9th Divs.; there was also the 13th Transport Flight of the RHAF, which helped evacuate US X Corps from Hŭngnam. The 849-strong battalion, with headquarters, HQ company, and three rifle companies each with one MG mortar and three rifle platoons, reached Pusan on 9 December 1950, and joined US 7th Cav.Regt. (US 1st Cav.Div.). On 29 January 1951 the battalion captured Hill 402, and,

[1]The World War II *nom de guerre* of Lt.Col. Magrin-Vernerey, who led the Foreign Legion's 13^e Demi-Brigade at Narvik and in East Africa. Like many of De Gaulle's small band of officers from the years of exile, he kept his wartime pseudonym—e.g. Gen. Leclerc.

on 5 October occupied Hill 313 ('Scotch Hill'), losing 28 dead. In January 1952 they patrolled with 15th Inf. (US 3rd Div.); and in May they helped guard Koje-do camp. Finally, in June 1953, they held 'Harry Hill' against determined Chinese assaults. On 13 January 1954 the arrival of 1,667 reinforcements enabled expansion to the two-battalion Hellenic Regiment. By the end of 1955 almost all had left Korea, having lost 182 dead.

On 31 January 1951 the **Belgium–Luxemburg** contribution—the 1st Belgian Bn. (Bataillon Belge)—arrived at Pusan, comprising a headquarters, HQ company, and heavy weapons company (all mixed Walloon/Flemish); A and B (rifle)

Four soldiers of Princess Patricia's Canadian Light Infantry pose cheerfully with Communist propaganda placards. All wear the Canadian summer-weight field caps; the two foreground veterans both display Canadian parachute wings; the corporal (left front) has chevrons stencilled in miniature beside his cap badge, imitating US practice; the man at right rear has a Canadian-issued US-made olive brown sweater. The Corporal's battledress blouse is British 1946 issue, worn with winter overtrousers; the man at right front wears Canadian battledress, and US combat boots. His .303 Lee Enfield was the standard rifle throughout Commonwealth contingents. (Public Archives Canada)

Companies (Walloon), and C Co. (Flemish). The Luxemburg Detachment of 48 men formed the 1st Ptn. of A Co., and wore the Grand-Ducal monogram on the collar patches of their Belgian uniforms. The battalion fought magnificently at the Imjin River, supporting British 29th Bde.; it was relieved on 21 August by the 2nd Bn., which was then assigned to US 7th Inf.Regt. (3rd Div.). In October this unit defended a forward position at Haktang-ni for three days against a heavy Chinese attack. From 26 March 1952 to 20 January 1953 the 2nd Luxemburg Ptn. served with the battalion. In April 1953 the unit fought off Chinese attacks at Chatkol. In June 1955 the last Belgians left Korea, having lost 103 dead (including two Luxemburgers).

Emperor Haile Selassie, eager to involve **Ethiopia** in the internationalised conflict, sent the 1st Kagnew ('Conquerors') Bn., formed in August 1950 with three rifle companies (1st, 2nd and 4th Cos.) drawn from his élite Imperial Guard. They arrived at Pusan on 7 May 1951, and joined US 32nd Inf.Regt. (7th Div.) on 'Line Kansas'. From 16 to 22 September they were engaged in furious hand-to-hand fighting at Sam-Hyon. On 29 March 1952 2nd Kagnew Bn. took over, to be relieved in its turn on 16 April 1953 by 3rd Kagnew Bn., which drove off at bayonet-point a Chinese attack at Tokan-ni on 20 May. This unit was fighting at Pork Chop Hill at the time of the Armistice. The last Ethiopian soldier left Korea on 3 January 1965.

In 1950 **Colombia** sent the frigate *Almirante Padilla*, followed on 15 June 1951 by the 1st Colombia Bn. (Batallón Colombia), the only Latin American ground unit ever to fight in Asia. Colombians were fined five dollars for not shaving daily or writing home weekly, and a nine-piece Latin band accompanied them; but this was no 'operetta army', for they earned a fighting reputation surpassed only by the Turks. The 1,060-strong reinforced battalion joined US 24th Div. and first saw combat on 7 August, later mounting an epic defence of Kumsong from 13 to 23 October. In early 1952 they transferred to the US 31st Inf. (US 7th Div.); and fought on 'Old Baldy' before being relieved by the 2nd Bn. on 4 July. After the fight for 'T-Bone Hill' in late 1952 the 3rd Bn. took over, also fighting at 'Old Baldy' before relief by 4th Bn. on 25 June 1953. By the time this battalion left Korea in October 1954, 131 Colombians had died in action.

The first foreign medical team to arrive in Korea was from the **Swedish** Red Cross, operating a field hospital at Pusan from 23 September 1950 until 10 April 1957. On 7 March 1951 the **Danish** Red Cross ship *Jutlandia* anchored in Pusan harbour, and operated there and at Inchon with 100 medical personnel until 16 August 1957. From May 1951 until 1954 the **Norwegian** Red Cross (after 1 November 1951, the Norwegian Army) operated 'Normash', a Mobile Army Surgical Hospital ('Mash'), the 106 personnel wearing at first Norwegian and later US Army uniforms. Finally,

Men of the 3rd Turkish Bde. arrive in the Panbudong sector to take over from the 3/7th US Marines in May 1953. By this date the Turks were entirely clothed and equipped with US items, including the US Army's nylon/aluminium 'Armor, Vest, M12'. (US Army courtesy Simon Dunstan)

North Korean KPA:
1: Sergeant, summer field dress, 1950
2: Private, winter field dress, 1950
3: Colonel, service dress, 1952

A

Republic of Korea:
1: Major, service dress, 1950
2: Lieutenant, field dress, 1950
3: Trained Private, winter field dress, 1950

B

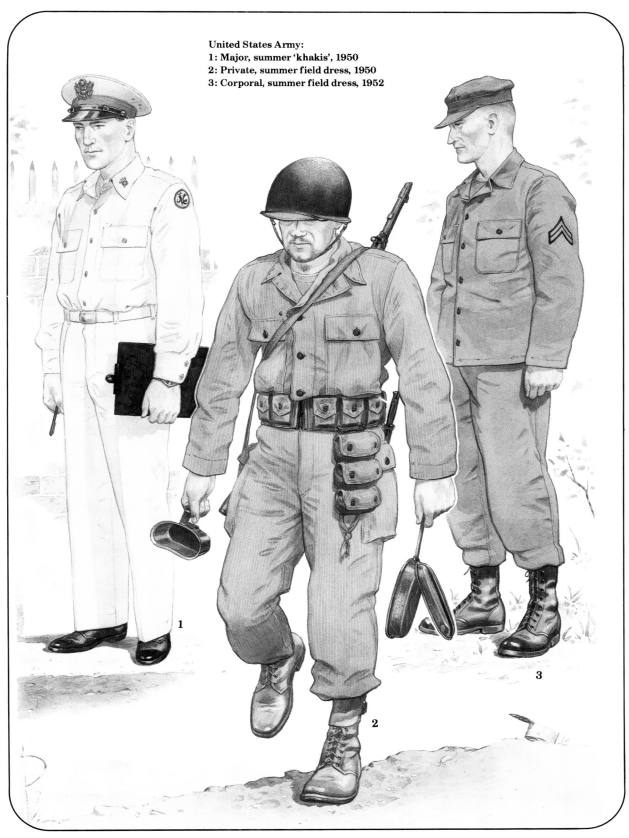

United States Army:
1: Major, summer 'khakis', 1950
2: Private, summer field dress, 1950
3: Corporal, summer field dress, 1952

C

1: US Army Sgt., field dress, 1951
2: US Marine, winter field dress, 1953
3: Lt.Col., Colombian contingent, 1953

D

1: Cpl., 3rd Bn., Royal Australian Regt., 1950
2: Pte., 1st Bn., The Gloucestershire Regt. (UK), 1951
3: Sgt., Royal 22ᵉ Régiment (Canada), 1951

E

1: Lt., Bn. de Corée (France), 1951
2: Kpl. l^eKl., Regt. Van Heutsz (Netherlands), 1951
3: Capt., Bataillon Belge, 1950

F

1: Major, Turkish Bde., 1950
2: Lt., 1st Kagnew Bn. (Ethiopia), 1951
3: L/Cpl., 21st Inf. Regt. (Thailand), 1951

G

Chinese People's Liberation Army:
1: Infantryman, winter field dress, 1950
2: Infantryman, summer field dress, 1951
3: Officer, service dress, 1952

H

from 16 November 1951 until 2 January 1955, the **Italian** Red Cross built and ran a hospital at Yongdungpo.

People's Republic of China

In 1950 the Chinese People's Liberation Army (*Chung-Kuo Jen-Min Chieh-Fang Chün*—hereafter PLA), comprising the Army, Navy, Air Force and Militia of the year-old People's Republic, was commanded by the Minister of Defence, Chu-Teh, Army commander since June 1930. There were between two and three million troops in four Field Armies (numbered 1st–4th) and GHQ units (sometimes called 5th Field Army); and one to two million in the second-line Garrison Armies. A Field Army (130,000–160,000 strong, equivalent to a weak US or British 'army') contained about three Group Armies (1st–23rd). A Group Army (30,000–80,000 strong, equivalent to a Western 'corps') usually contained two to six Armies (1st–about 77th). The Army (21,000–30,000 strong, or half again the size of a US or British Division) was the principal self-sufficient tactical formation. Each comprised three, sometimes four, Divisions (numbered 1st–about 230th); artillery, special duty, training and lorry transport regiments; and engineer, reconnaissance, communications and anti-aircraft battalions. A division (7,000–10,000 strong, equivalent to a US 'light division') had three infantry regiments (1st–about 700th), an artillery regiment, and engineer, transport, medical and signals companies. A regiment (in theory 3,242 men, but usually understrength) had three infantry battalions (each with three three-platoon companies), an artillery battery, and guard, mortar, transport, signals, medical and stretcher companies. There were also some artillery divisions (with artillery and rocket-projector regiments), and Inner Mongolian mounted cavalry divisions, but apparently no armoured divisions at this time, although the PLA did operate some ex-Nationalist tanks. Army organisation was strictly triangular, and all regiments were allocated to divisions in numerical sequence, as were divisions to armies.

Although 3,000 recently arrived Soviet military

Lt.Col. M. P. A. den Ouden, the first CO of the Netherlands Bn., decorates men of his command with the US Bronze Star. Note the US-style green 'combat leader' loops worn on his shoulder straps. Den Ouden was killed in action near Hungsong on 12 February 1951. (Mil.Hist.Sec., Royal Dutch Army)

advisers were training the PLA in modern mechanised warfare, it was still at this stage a mass infantry force unsurpassed in its experience of guerrilla warfare. The Army was multi-racial, with a cadre of dedicated Communists controlling ex-nationalist deserters and PoWs, and troops from the compromised Chinese, Manchukuo and Mongol collaborationist armies. To prevent élitism 'positional titles' (or 'appointments') were substituted for the usual military ranks (see table). Equipment was poor, and logistical services rudimentary, but the calibre of the ordinary soldier made the PLA a formidable fighting machine.

The North Korean invasion of the South had come as a surprise to Peking, but the Chinese were unwilling to see the destruction of a fellow Communist state when the tide of war began to turn against it. By 14 October 1950 the first regular PLA troops—designated 'Chinese People's Volunteers', to disguise official Chinese entry into the war, and commanded by 'General' P'eng Teh-huai—had crossed the Yalu River secretly into North Korea. By early November these comprised 200,000 men in the 13th Group Army (38th, 39th, 40th Armies); 42nd, 50th and 66th Armies; 8th Artillery and 1st

and 2nd Motorised Artillery Divisions; a cavalry regiment, and the 42nd Motor Transport Regiment.

They promptly smashed ROK forces at the Chosin Reservoir, but 38th and 40th Armies sustained heavy losses at Ch'ongch'on against US IX Corps before attacking the weaker ROK II Corps. On 27 November 9th Group Army (20th, 26th, 27th Armies) was so badly mauled in its unsuccessful attempt to prevent US X Corps' fighting retreat to Hŭngnam that it was withdrawn to Manchuria for re-organisation. Meanwhile the main Chinese force (38th, 39th, 40th, 42nd, 50th, 66th Armies) chased the remaining US/ROK forces out of North Korea, pausing in December at the 38th Parallel. Then, on 1 January 1951, they surged southwards, and occupied Seoul before halting for resupply. The crude logistical 'tail' was

Belgian and Greek troops attached to US 3rd Infantry Div., 1951, with GIs wearing that division's insignia on their helmets. The Greeks have a national flag insignia on their helmets; the beret-wearing Belgians are armed with the M49 FN automatic rifle. (Royal Belgian Embassy)

Appointments in the Chinese PLA

Title	Literal Translation	British Equivalent
Yen-chan-chün Ssu-ling-yüan	Field Army Commanding Officer	General
Ping-t'uan Ssu-ling yüan	Group Army Commanding Officer	Lieut. General
Chün Ssu-ling-yüan	Army Commanding Officer	Major General
Shih Ssu-ling-yüan	Divisional Commanding Officer	Brigadier
Shih Fu Ssu-ling-yüan	Deputy Divisional Commanding Officer	Brigadier
T'uan-chang	Regimental Commander	Colonel
Fu T'uan-chang	Deputy Regimental Commander	Lieut. Colonel
Ying-chang	Battalion Commander	Major
Lien-chang	Company Commander	Captain
Fu Lien-chang	Deputy Company Commander	Lieutenant
P'ai-chang	Platoon Commander	2nd Lieutenant
Fu P'ai-chang	Deputy Platoon Commander	Sergeant
Pan-chang	Section Commander	Corporal
Fu Pan-chang	Deputy Section Commander	Lance-Corporal
Chan-shih	Fighter	Private

On 16 September 1955 (with effect 1 January 1956) this system was replaced by Soviet-style ranks. Under the Cultural Revolution it was reinstated, with the addition of 'Chieh-fang Chün Tsung-ssu-ling'—Commander-in-Chief of the PLA—equivalent to Field Marshal. On 1 August 1983 a return to Soviet-style ranks was announced.

quite unable to supply even the modest 40 tons of supplies needed by a Chinese division (a US Division needed 600!) after so rapid an advance. On 11 February 40th, 66th and KPA 5th Armies pressed on towards Wonju, using massed 'human wave' tactics for the first time; but these caused appalling casualties in the face of the deadly UN firepower, and the Chinese were forced to retreat back over the 38th Parallel, having lost Seoul.

Now seven more armies (12th, 15th, 47th, 60th, 63rd, 64th, 65th) arrived for the First Spring Offensive, which was to be the PLA's greatest (if ultimately unsuccessful) effort of the war. In the west, the 3rd and 19th Group Armies would take Seoul; the 13th and reconstituted 19th Group Armies would attack in the central sector, backed up by independent Armies and even some Mongolian cavalry—a total of 30 divisions (250,000 men) with about 40 divisions in reserve. The offensive began on 22 April, but had already been halted by the 30th, with 70,000 casualties, Seoul still out of reach, and the advance in the central sector blunted after 40 miles by the stand of 29th British Bde. at the Imjin. On 17 May pressure switched to the east in the Second Spring Offensive, with 21 Chinese divisions and two North Korean armies, led by 3rd and 9th Group Armies; but after four days and 90,000 casualties the advance petered out. The Chinese were shattered, and realised that even their virtually unlimited human resources could not overcome the murderous UN firepower. They retreated as the UN counter-attacked, to a secure line just inside North Korea, saved from humiliating defeat by UN reluctance to invade North Korea again, and by the hope of an armistice as peace talks opened.

The November 1951 stalemate found the Chinese troops manning static fortifications against an enemy who no longer feared them as invincible, but who did not wish to waste lives by attacking. Now the Chinese constructed a 14-mile-deep system of trenches, earthworks, deep tunnels and underground bases as shelter against artillery barrages, air strikes, and even nuclear attack. Using their unrivalled skills in concealment and camouflage, they moved only under cover of darkness, and attacked in battalion or company strength, supported by increased artillery, mortars and tanks. The Chinese now manned exclusively

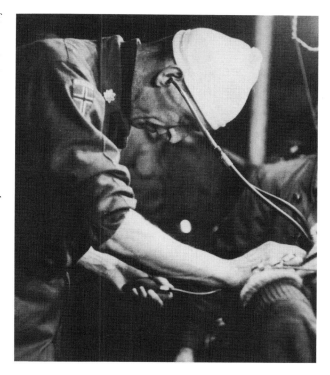

Dr E. Sandaa, commander of NORMASH, carries out an operation. Note US rank insignia, and national shoulder patch—'NORGE' over the Norwegian flag. (Royal Norwegian Embassy)

the western and central sectors, facing UN/ROK forces, leaving the relatively peaceful eastern sector to their weaker North Korean allies. Their probing attacks, usually against vulnerable ROK units, were localised but still vicious: in January 1952 they lost 4,000 men in a single frenzied battle. In May 1952 they escalated attacks against 1st ROK Div., backed by artillery and mortar barrage, but were once again unsuccessful.

In July 1952 the CPV, now with 14 armies (12th, 15th, 20th, 26th, 27th, 38th, 39th, 40th, 42nd, 47th, 60th, 63rd–65th), began the 'Outpost Battles', but were usually repulsed, often with significant losses. In October they launched a major attack against US IX Corps, but lost 2,000 men from 38th Army in two days. Activity declined over the winter months, and more armies arrived as reinforcements (16th, 24th, 54th, 67th and 68th). Now there were seven Chinese and two North Korean armies in the line, 270,000 men, and 11 armies with a further 531,000 in reserve. In March 1953 the Chinese attacked hard in the west towards Seoul; and in mid-June a major assault in the central sector

Chinese troops cross the Yalu River in October 1950 to drive back the victorious United Nations troops.

pushed ROK II Corps back three miles. On 13 July the Chinese attacked in the centre again, but lost a staggering 72,000 men—equivalent to two armies—before the Armistice brought fighting to a close.

P'eng Teh-huai's Chinese People's Volunteers returned home in triumph; in October 1954 P'eng was promoted Minister of Defence, and in September 1955 he became one of ten newly-created 'Marshals of the People's Republic of China'. (In September 1959 he was dismissed after a quarrel with Mao.) The PLA, in spite of 900,000 losses, was now Asia's most powerful army, and it embarked on a massive modernisation programme to match the firepower of the now pathologically hated Americans.

The order of battle of the CPV was as follows (*indicates formations present in July 1953; u/i means unidentified):

1st Army* (1, 2, 7 Divs.) from 13th Gr. Army; 2nd Fd. Army

12th Army* (34 [later 31], 35, 36 Divs.) from 3rd Gr. Army; 2nd Fd. Army

15th Army* (29, 44, 45 Divs.) from 3rd Gr. Army; 2nd Fd. Army

16th Army (46, 47, 48 [later 46, 47, u/i, 32] Divs.) from 9th Gr. Army

20th Army (58, 59, 60, 89 Divs.) from 9th Gr. Army; 3rd Fd. Army

23rd Army* (67, 69, 73 Divs.) from 9th Gr. Army

24th Army* (70, 72, 77 [later 74] Divs.) from 9th Gr. Army

26th Army (76, 77, 78, 88 Divs.) from 9th Gr. Army; 3rd Fd. Army

27th Army (79, 80, 81, 90 Divs.) from 9th Gr. Army; 3rd Fd. Army

38th Army* (112, 113, 114 Divs.) from 13th Gr. Army; 4th Fd. Army

39th Army* (115, 116, 117 Divs.) from 13th Gr. Army; 4th Fd. Army

40th Army* (118, 119, 120 Divs.) from 13th Gr. Army; 4th Fd. Army

41st Army (121, 122, 123 Divs.)

42nd Army (124, 125, 126 Divs.) from 14th Gr. Army; 4th Fd. Army

46th Army* (133, 136, 137, Divs.) from 13th Gr. Army

47th Army* (139, 140, 141 Divs.) from 13th Gr. Army; 4th Fd. Army

50th Army* (148, 149, 150 Divs.) from 13th Gr. Army; 4th Fd. Army

54th Army* (160, 161, 162 [later 130, 132, 135] Divs.) from 20th Gr. Army

60th Army* (178 [later 33, 181], 179, 180 Divs.) from 3rd Gr. Army; 2nd Fd. Army

63rd Army* (187, 188, 189 Divs.) from 19th Gr. Army; 1st Fd. Army

64th Army* (190, 191, 192 Divs.) from 19th Gr. Army; 1st Fd. Army

65th Army* (193, 194, 195 Divs.) from 19th Gr. Army; 1st Fd. Army

66th Army (196, 197, 198 Divs.) from 1st Fd. Army

A Chinese defensive position—note elderly Maxim-type machine gun, and bottle-shaped stick grenade.

67th Army* (199, 200, 201 Divs.) from 20th Gr.
  Army
68th Army* (202, 203, 204 Divs.) from 20th Gr.
  Army
70th Army (208, 209, 210 Divs.)

Also present in July 1953: four motorised artillery divs., 1st (25, 26, 27 Regts.), 2nd (28, 29, 30 Regts.), 7th (11, 20, 21 Regts.), 8th (31, 44, 45, 47, 48 Regts.); 21st Rocket Launcher Div. (201, 202, 203 Regts.); six anti-tank regts. (401–406); five horse-drawn artillery regts. (9, 10, 40, 41, u/i); four AA regts. (1, 2, 3, 9) and four tank regts. (1, 6 and two u/i).

The Plates

A: North Korean KPA

A1: Sergeant, summer field dress, 1950

The Russian-style shirt/blouse was often worn inside the trousers, with the collar unfastened and the opening filled by a separate triangular 'gas flap' of blue cloth. A simplified version introduced later in the war had plain cuffs, and only one flapless pocket on the left breast. The baggy trousers were fastened with tapes at the ankle and worn with rubber-soled canvas ankle boots. The original olive khaki shade faded rapidly to a light yellowish hue. The detachable shoulder boards were made of a superior material which retained its dark olive green colour better and contrasted markedly with the rest of the uniform: some, at least, could be reversed to act as red or green full dress insignia. The uniform had reinforcing patches on the elbows, trouser seat and knees, and frequently single or double rows of horizontal 'zigzag' stitching around the cap and across the shoulders, chest and upper sleeves, which were used to hold leaf camouflage. The Soviet-style steel helmet had the national badge painted on the front, but seems to have been little worn in the field.

Tank crews appear to have worn Russian-style one-piece overalls in black or khaki, with high boots and padded canvas helmets.

A2: Private, winter dress, 1950

This quilted cotton uniform was padded with

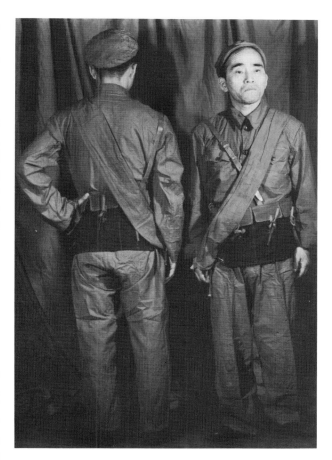

Japanese employees of the US Army model the Chinese People's Volunteers' cotton summer combat uniform—cf. Plate H. The fabric tube slung around the body is for carrying rations; the mixed leather and fabric pouch rig is that also shown in the posed photo on page 3. (US Army via Lee Russell)

cotton wool or kapok. The style followed that of the summer uniform, except that the shirt/blouse had a low standing collar. The field cap, which was made from the same material, had larger side flaps which could be fastened under the chin but were otherwise tied over the crown. The uniform was worn with padded mittens which had separate thumbs and trigger fingers, and rubber-soled ankle boots with quilted cotton tops. Some officers wore high boots of white felt which had a strip of dark leather all the way up the front. There was also a double-breasted parka with slanting side pockets; and officers had conventional double-breasted greatcoats with Soviet-style collar tabs. Later the blouse was replaced by a five-button double-breasted jacket similar to that of the Chinese PLA; some, indeed, may have been of Chinese origin, for the North

Korean supply position must have been severely affected by the UN's 1950 advance. Equipment resembled the Soviet World War II pattern, with leather waist belts and ammunition pouches, and a plain canvas rucksack and haversack. The armament was identical to the current Soviet issue, and consisted of SKS carbines or PPSh41 SMGs.

A3: Colonel, service dress, 1952

This smart, Russian-style uniform seems to date from 1948 at least. The tunic was very similar to the 1943 Soviet *kittel* except in having pointed cuffs. The piping was red for the Army and green for the Border Constabulary. The tunic was almost always worn with Russian-style breeches and high black boots, though long trousers seem to have been authorised for undress. The North Koreans appear to have followed the Soviet practice whereby both wore dark blue for parade and walking-out dress and khaki for field service. Generals had broad double arm-of-service colour stripes, and other officers narrow piping. All ranks wore the distinctive North Korean cap, but only officers had the piping around the crown and the two diagonal lines on either side of the badge. The badge itself clearly reflected Soviet influence, as did the shoulder boards. The officers' field uniform was similar except that it was made of cotton drill and lacked the piping. There was also a white summer tunic in the same style, which was worn with the peaked cap and blue or khaki trousers. The dress tunic was worn without a belt, the field version with a 'Sam Browne' with a plain frame buckle.

B: Army of the Republic of Korea
B1: Major, service dress, 1950

The Republic of Korea's Army was organised under American auspices, and received surplus US arms, equipment and uniforms from 1947 onwards. ROK officers wore the US Army's olive drab tunic and trousers; its summer service dress of light khaki shirt and trousers; or, as in this case, the battledress-

NORTH KOREAN ARMY INSIGNIA:
(1) *Cap badge*—red & gold. **(2)** *Won-su*, **field marshal**—Kim Il-Sung only. **(3)** *Ch'a-su*, **deputy field marshal**—rank not held at this date. **(4)** *Sang-jang*, **lieutenant-general.** NB, the four-star rank of *Tae-jang*, **general**, is not shown here. **(5)** *Chung-jang*, **major-general.** **(6)** *So-jang*, **brigadier.** **(7)** *Tae-jwa*, **senior colonel.** **(8)** *Sang-jwa*, **colonel**—here, Armour. **(9)** *Chung-jwa*, **lieutenant-colonel**—Artillery. **(10)** *So-jwa*, **major**—Engineers. **(11)** *Tae-wi*, **senior captain**—Medical. **(12)** *Sang-wi*, **captain**—Signals. **(13)** *Chung-wi*, **lieutenant**—Judge Advocate's Dept. **(14)** *So-wi*, **second lieutenant.** **(15)** *T'ŭng-mu Sang-sa*, **warrant officer, sergeant-major.** **(16)** *Sang-sa*, **staff sergeant.** **(17)** *Chung-sa*, **sergeant.** **(18)** *Ha-sa*, **corporal.** **(19)** *Sang-dŭng*, **lance-corporal.** **(20)** *Chŏn-sa*, **private.**

Officers' shoulder boards were in broad gold (combat arms) or narrow silver lace (services), with contrasting stars; the piping was red in the Army and green in the Border Constabulary. NCOs' straps were olive green with gold bars and red or green piping. (P. Abbott)

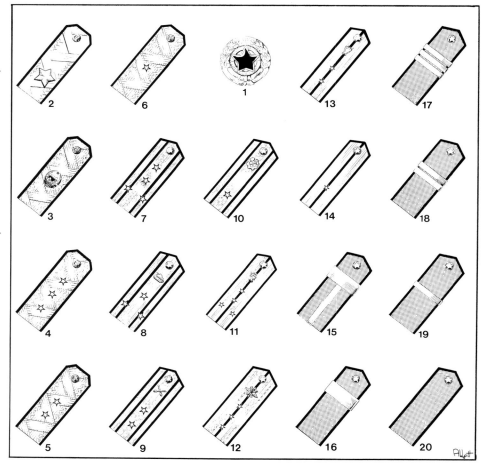

Sgt. 1st Class Frank R. Oakes, Lt.Col. Francis Deisher and Lt. Roe Byong Heon supervising repatriation of Communist PoWs at Panmunjom in August 1953—thus the supervisor's arm brassards. Note minor differences in the fatigue patterns (see commentaries to Plates C, D); and methods of wearing rank and branch insignia, USA and ROK. (US Army via Lee Russell)

style 'Eisenhower jacket' which had become the standard US temperate climate service dress garment during the immediate post-war period. US officers could combine it with light-coloured slacks on the same basis as the pre-war 'pinks and greens', and this officer has obviously followed their example. A closed-collar version, worn with olive drab trousers and peaked cap, was authorised for enlisted men. The cap badge featured the traditional *yang* and *yin* symbol. While generals wore US-style stars, field and company grade officers wore their devices mounted on gilt backing bars in a fashion reminiscent of World War II Japanese practice, and the service dress tunic sometimes bore Japanese-style cuff braiding. US-style arm-of-service devices existed by the end of the war, and were supposed to be worn on the left hand side of the shirt collar after the US fashion, but few photographs actually show them in use. These branch devices were only worn by officers.

B2: Lieutenant, field dress, 1950
The North Korean invasion disrupted the ROK Army's supply system, and in the period before US material started to flood in, South Korean soldiers presented a very motley appearance. Old Japanese Arisaka rifles and even some steel helmets were brought out of store, and many troops had to make do with canvas 'tennis shoes' instead of combat boots. The surplus US Army material supplied was not necessarily of the most up-to-date pattern. This officer, for instance, wears the US M41 field jacket, which had long been superseded in the US Army by the much improved M43 combat clothing. With it, he wears US-style olive drab woollen trousers, combat boots, and the peaked field cap of the summer fatigue uniform. Many ROK soldiers seem to have been issued with US Army greatcoats at the beginning of winter 1950–51, even though these were really obsolete as a field garment. By mid-1951, however, the South Koreans had been fully equipped with US-pattern field clothing. US influence extended to the development of a system of divisional patches, which were often painted on the helmet sides, and to parade embellishments such as chromed helmet liners, decorative cravats, and white ladder-lacing in the combat boots.

B3: Private, trained, winter field dress, 1950
Although the South Koreans wore what were essentially US uniforms, there were certain differences. The US M42 HBT summer fatigues sometimes had the same 'zigzag' stitching across the upper part of the blouse as appeared on North Korean uniforms and which were apparently designed to hold foliage camouflage. This NCO is wearing an indigenous winter outfit made of the same quilted cotton material as the North Korean and Chinese models (which seems sometimes to have led to cases of mistaken identity, with ROK stragglers being taken for Communists by their UN allies); it differed in that the material was olive green in colour, generally with a criss-cross quilting pattern, and in having two large breast pockets like the M42 HBT fatigue jacket. It was often worn with a US-pattern pile cap instead of the steel helmet. Like the belt, web pouches and combat boots, this was of the standard US World War II pattern. Rank chevrons were supposed to be worn on the upper arms, but this seems to have been rare on the field clothing; they more commonly appeared on the helmet front, sometimes with miniature versions on the left hand breast pocket flap.

C: United States Army
C1: Major, summer khakis, 1950

The term 'khaki' can cause confusion because Americans use it to mean a light tan, whereas to the British and others it means a darker shade more akin to the American olive drab. During the 1930s the practice of wearing khaki shirts and privately purchased trousers developed; and these became issue garments for enlisted men in 1938–40, along with the 'overseas cap', until then not authorised for wear in the United States. This practical and comfortable hot-weather uniform was also widely worn by officers; it continued to be the main summer service dress after 1945, and was worn in rear areas, such as Japan, throughout the Korean War. Officers and warrant officers were also authorised to purchase a khaki tunic as an optional item for wear on more formal occasions. The style was similar to that of the olive drab tunic, except that the lower pocket flaps were pointed, and it lacked a cloth belt. After World War II some officers began to wear a khaki version of the 'Ike jacket' instead of the tunic, though this garment seems to have been less common than its olive drab

ROK ARMY INSIGNIA:
(1) Infantry. (2) Artillery. (3) Medical. (4) Armour—all the foregoing, gold. (5) Engineers—silver, gold star. (6) Cap badge—red/blue centre with silver petals, gold wreath. (7) I Corps—dark blue and white. (8) Capitol Division—green shield, white rim, yellow tiger's head. (9) 1st Division—dark blue rims, yellow shield, red numeral. (10) 3rd Division—dark blue and white. (11) *Chung-jang*, lieutenant-general. (12) *So-jang*, major-general. (13) *Chun-jang*, brigadier—all the foregoing, silver. (14) *Tae-ryŏng*, colonel. (15) *Chung-ryong*, lieutenant-colonel. (16) *So-ryŏng*, major—all foregoing, gold bars, light and dark silver roundels; one US source gives red and blue roundels, possibly full dress. (17) *Tae-wi*, captain. (18) *Chung-wi*, lieutenant. (19) *So-wi*, second lieutenant—all foregoing, silver bars on gold. (20) *T'ŭng-mu Sang-sa*, warrant officer, sergeant-major. (21) *I-dŭng Sang-sa*, sergeant. (22) *Il-tŭng Chung-sa*, lance-sergeant. (23) *I-dŭng Chung-sa*, corporal. (24) *Ha-sa*, lance-corporal. (25) *Il-tŭng Pyong*, trained private. All chevrons, white on green. Not shown are the ranks of *Tae-jang*, four-star general, not held at that period; *Chun-wi*, senior warrant officer, who wore a plain gold bar on the shoulder strap; *Il-t'ŭng Sang-sa*, a senior NCO rank junior to (20) and lacking the star; and I-dŭng Ryong (Recruit), no insignia.

From 15 May 1954 field and company officers' insignia changed from the illustrated April 1946 models to sequences of silver blossoms and diamonds. (P. Abbott)

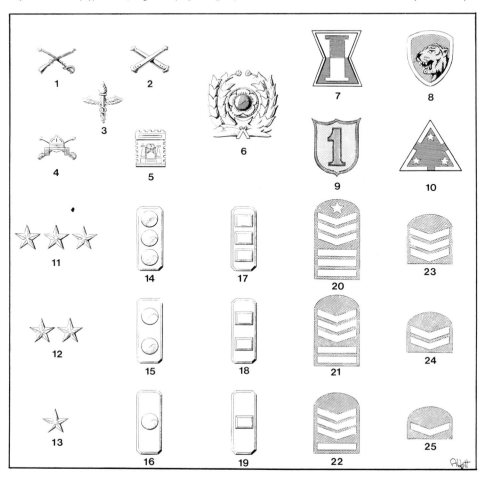

equivalent. Insignia were the same on all uniforms: here, Quartermaster Corps, Japan Logistical Command.

US troops advance on Taegu during the offensive following the Inchon landings in autumn 1950; apart from the hessian helmet covers—and the 'brewed' T-34/85 tank of the KPA's 105th Armd.Bde.—there is nothing to distinguish this scene from many taken in the latter stages of the Pacific War against Japan.

C2: Soldier, summer field dress, 1950

Among the most important of the US Army's innovations during World War II was the use of fatigue clothing as hot-weather combat dress. The first fatigues used in this way were the M41 HBT (Herring Bone Twill) work suits, which could be recognised by their hip-length jackets and shirt-type cuffs. These were occasionally to be seen in Korea; but were largely superseded by the two-piece M42 fatigues, which differed in having a longer coat with tab closures at the cuffs, a gas flap across the neck opening (almost always removed in practice), and unusually large 'bellows' pockets on the chest and high on the hips of the trousers. With these fatigues went a peaked field cap, whose short visor was lengthened after 1945. The HBT material was tough and hardwearing, but it was also heavy and slow to dry when wet. It presented a faintly 'striped' appearance, though this was only visible close up. The original colour was a dark green (Army Shade 7) which quickly faded to a pale greenish grey. These garments became the basis for the Army's post-war summer combat dress, and were widely worn in Korea by the US Army, ROK and other UN troops.

C3: Corporal, summer field dress, 1952

During the second year of the war the M42 HBT fatigues began to be replaced by a newer pattern. These appear to have been designed in 1947 but not manufactured until the early 1950s. The coat resembled that of the M42 set and had the same gas flap (again, almost invariably removed), but the cuffs were plain, and the pockets were of the normal patch type with squared-off flaps and 'docked' bottoms. The trousers had normal side and back pockets, and the buttons were of plain plastic instead of being the earlier '13 star' black metal pattern. The first batches of these new fatigues were made of the old HBT cloth, but later ones were of dark olive green (OG 107) cotton twill. Like all

'Chow' in the snow: members of HQ Co., 2nd Bn., 8th Cavalry display various types of fatigues, mainly M43 pattern, and pile caps worn on top of fatigue caps. (US Army)

Korean War fatigues, they were baggy and shapeless. Those worn in the field seldom bore formation patches or even rank chevrons, though smartened-up versions worn with decorative neckerchiefs, highly polished or chromed helmet liners and white ladder-laced combat boots began to appear behind the lines. Like many line NCOs, this corporal has retained the older World War II-style chevrons instead of the unpopular 1948-pattern miniatures (blue on gold for combatant arms, gold on blue for services) which were discontinued early in 1951.

D1: Sergeant, US Army, field dress, 1951
The US Army retained its successful M43 field uniform after World War II. The material was windproof cotton sateen in a distinctly greenish shade of olive drab. In summer the jacket could be worn over the HBT fatigues. In winter the jacket and trousers were worn over a woollen shirt, sweater and 'liner' (a woollen cardigan-style garment) in a browner shade of olive drab. The M43 peaked field cap had ear flaps, but the pile cap more commonly accompanied this uniform during the Korean winter. The World War II 'double-buckle' combat boots were progressively replaced by plain lace-up ones, all in russet leather. This M43 uniform equipped the majority of US troops in Korea, as well as the re-equipped ROK troops and many of the UN contingents. However, it began to give way to an improved version known as the M51. The jacket differed only in having snap pocket closures instead of buttons; but the trousers had the

side 'cargo' pockets previously used only by paratroops, and the shirt and sweater were dark green. The practice of adding a rigid liner to the M51 field cap produced the fashionable, képi-like 'Walker' or 'Ridgway' cap typical of the later 1950s and '60s. This NCO wears the 1948-pattern miniature chevrons, just visible on the right.

D2: US Marine, winter dress, 1953
The US Marines wore their own HBT 'utilities', peaked field cap and camouflaged helmet cover, and retained the early World War II-pattern ankle boots and canvas leggings, which led the North Koreans to nickname them 'yellowlegs'. Their winter uniforms approximated more to the Army pattern, however, and included M43 jackets, trousers and pile caps, together with World War II parkas, and the unsatisfactory canvas and rubber 'shoepaks'. The M51 winter outfit was issued to both arms, although not until relatively late in the war. It was based on the same 'layering' principle as the M43. The field jacket and trousers were worn over frieze liners, which were white and dark green respectively; a green flannel shirt; and a loose-fitting white undershirt and drawers. For really cold weather a parka and overtrousers could be added. The parka resembled the World War II pattern except that it lacked a belt, had only the slanting upper pockets, and was olive green instead of the earlier light tan. The boots were of double-thickness rubber with a layer of felt between: perspiration was prevented from evaporating, but the insulation supposedly kept it from freezing. There were leather gloves with woollen inserts, or Arctic mittens which had pile backs for rubbing frostbitten noses and faces.

D3: Teniente Coronel, Colombian contingent, 1953
This is a good example of the 'smartened-up' fatigues worn by most senior officers during the Korean War. Non-Commonwealth UN contingents normally wore standard US field clothing with the addition of their own national and rank insignia (this did not apply to the Filipino troops, who were still using US-style rank insignia at this period), usually with the patch of the US Division to which they were attached on their left shoulders. This lieutenant-colonel wears the M47-pattern fatigue blouse with M42-pattern trousers, a mixture

of styles which was entirely characteristic of the period. For some reason he has the Colombian national badge under the title 'COLOMBIA' in gold on red in place of a divisional patch. The same badge has been sewn to his neckerchief (a post-war US Army fashion) whose light blue could stand both for the United Nations or infantry in the US service. Colombian company officers wore one to three gilt stars, and field officers similar stars with a gilt bar: since the fatigue jackets lacked shoulder straps this officer has presumably pinned his insignia (two stars divided by a bar) to the collar in the US fashion, adding the conventional crossed rifles of his arm-of-service device on the left.

E1: Australia: Corporal, 3rd Bn., Royal Australian Regiment, 1950

The Australian contingent was initially equipped with the familiar loosely fitting tunic, trousers and 'Digger' hat worn in two world wars, and a summer uniform of khaki drill shirt and trousers. Black boots had replaced brown in 1948. The canvas gaiters resembled the American pattern but were fastened with straps, while other web equipment followed British models. White-on-red 'ROYAL AUSTRALIAN REGIMENT' shoulder titles replaced the discontinued battalion patches, but the RAR's regimental badge did not supplant the well-known 'Rising Sun' until 1954. The Australians were the first Commonwealth troops to receive US winter clothing. This included pile caps, on which they were ordered to wear 'Rising Sun' collar badges. In practice, many retained their distinctive wide-brimmed headgear—as one said, 'They can take away my strides, but not my hat.' Steel helmets were conspicuous by their absence. Subsequently, British-pattern proofed combat dress and steel helmets and US flak jackets were adopted for field wear. The original service dress uniform was replaced by 1948-pattern Australian battledress, which differed little from the British model except that the lapels were rather wider. The distinctive hat and gaiters were retained, and 2nd RAR initiated the Australian practice of blackening the latter in 1952.

E2: Great Britain: Private, 1st Bn., The Gloucestershire Regiment, 1951

The British arrived wearing 1950-pattern jungle

Pfc. David W. Jackson of Co.L, 5th RCT, wearing the early 'Vest, Armored, M-1951' in late September 1952. By this date the US Army had received some 20,000 examples of this USMC-procured vest; the first shipment of the Army's own 'Armor, Vest, M-1952' did not arrive until that December. Early reports indicated that the use of body armour reduced the casualties by about 30 per cent. For full details see MAA 157, Flak Jackets. (US Army courtesy Simon Dunstan)

green bush shirts, trousers and floppy bush hats. At the onset of winter they donned standard khaki serge battledress and cap comforters, later 'acquiring' US M43 combat clothing. Meanwhile, supplies of British World War II-pattern cold weather clothing were rushed out. This included string vests, long underwear, ribbed sweaters, oiled socks, felt-lined boots, visored field caps with neck and ear flaps, gloves, gauntlets and the 1942 windproof outer suit consisting of a hooded smock and overtrousers in a green, brown and khaki 'brushed' camouflage pattern. For the second winter they were issued with a newly designed field uniform of greenish grey gaberdine, consisting of combat jacket, trousers, peaked field cap, inner and outer parkas and rubber-soled boots. The cap (dubbed 'Hat, Horrible') was not a success, but the jacket and trousers went on to become the M58 combat

Chef de bataillon (**Major**) **Barthélémy, adjutant of the French battalion, newly awarded the US Legion of Merit. Like many veterans of Free French service with the British, he retains the British right-hand beret 'pull'. He wears American shirt and trousers, a French 1946 brown leather belt, cloth French shoulder strap ranking, and a mixture of French, US and ROK decorations and insignia. Note the** NATIONS UNIES **tricolour shield badge worn on the collar. (E. C. P. Armées)**

UNITED NATIONS INSIGNIA:
(**1**) **Belgian Bn.** (**2**) **British 40th Div.**—initially worn by 27th Bde. (**3**) **British 29th Bde.** (**4**) **1st British Commonwealth Division.** (**5**) **25th Canadian Bde.** (**6**) **Colombian Bn.** (**7**) **Ethiopian Kagnew Bn.** (**8**) **French Bn.**—beret. (**9**) **Greek Bn.** (**10**) **Luxemburg Ptn.**—pocket patch. (**11**) **Netherlands Bn.** (**12**) **10th Philippines BCT.** (**13**) **Thai contingent.** (**14**) **Turkish Bde.**

dress. This private wears the Gloucesters' famous 'back badge' on his bush hat. The ribbed sweater was often worn as an outer garment, with the regimental title, divisional patch and rank chevrons on a drab brassard, and officers' pips sewn to the shoulders (and note this unit's US Citation clasp). The 1944 pattern Mk. 4 steel helmet became mandatory as enemy artillery strength increased, and US-supplied body armour made its appearance.

E3: Canada: Sergeant, Royal 22ᵉ Regiment, 1951
In 1950 the Canadian Army wore its own version of battledress, differing slightly from the British and made of a better-quality, rather greener material. Most units wore khaki berets, but the paratroop-trained 1st Battalions had maroon, and the armoured squadrons black. Summer wear consisted of a khaki flannel shirt or olive green bush jacket together with plain olive green 'bush pants'. Equipment followed the British pattern except that the web anklets were replaced by short puttees. Initially, the Canadians received US M43 jackets, overtrousers and US combat boots. Subsequently they introduced their own olive green nylon parka (in fact a hooded M43-style field jacket) and

overtrousers, together with a distinctively Canadian peaked field cap, which was manufactured in both wool and cotton. The earlier British Mk. 3 steel helmet was superseded by the later Mk. 4, with some US M1 helmets appearing towards the end. The Canadians wore their red brigade patch on both sleeves until they became part of the Commonwealth Division, after which they wore the latter's light blue shield on their left sleeve or brassard and their own patch on the right. Each regiment and corps had its own distinctively embroidered shoulder title. Rank insignia followed the standard British pattern at this period.

F1: France: Lieutenant, 1951
The Bataillon de Corée was raised in September 1950 from volunteers of all branches of the French army—Metropolitan, Colonial and Foreign Legion—and was commanded by Lt.Col. Olivier Le Mire, a former paratroop officer of the 1ᵉʳRCP. The mixed nature of the unit prompted him to organise the companies on 'tribal' lines: 1st Co. was largely composed of Colonials, 2nd of 'Metros', and 3rd of paratroopers from all three categories. The problem of distinctive headgear and insignia was solved by issuing the black beret of the para-

commando Bataillon de Choc. The use of enamelled beret and lapel (as opposed to pocket-fob) unit badges was a break with French tradition; the latter consisted of a tricolour shield with the inscription 'NATIONS UNIES'. The beret badge—illustrated elsewhere in detail—was usually, though not invariably, worn on the right; some berets also had two very prominent brass ventilation eyelets on the right side. Ranks were indicated on shoulder strap slides or chest tabs in the usual French manner.

On arrival in Korea the troops received US arms, equipment, combat clothing and steel helmets. The US 2nd Division's 'Indian Head' patch was worn; but they retained their French berets, and the lapel device occasionally appeared on fatigue dress collars. Ex-paras of the 3rd and HQ companies sometimes pinned their wings, or the French para beret badge, to the front flap of their pile caps; and some old North Africa hands sported the characteristic 'cheich' or desert scarf. Some paras kept their camouflaged smocks, often of ex-British stock, of the 1942 windproof winter suit, which was very popular for its lightness among French paras in Indochina at this period, and was nicknamed 'sausage skin'. The same smock was also issued to Commonwealth troops in Korea.

After returning to Indochina in October 1953, the unit formed the cadre for the two-battalion Régiment de Corée. (In June–July 1954 this was virtually wiped out in the Central Highlands of Vietnam, around An Khe and Pleiku, while serving with the famous Groupe Mobile 100.)

F2: Netherlands: Korporaal 1e Klasse, 1951

The volunteers were issued with the Dutch army's British-style battledress. Most wore standard khaki berets, but ex-paratroopers, Marines and cavalrymen retained their red, blue or black ones, bearing the brass badge of Regiment Van Heutsz (an eight-point star on a stylised 'W'), worn in the Dutch fashion on a distinctive ribbon backing, in this case black with orange edges. In Korea the volunteers received US fatigues for field wear and 'Ike' jackets and trousers for walking out; but the beret was commonly worn in preference to US headgear such as peaked fatigue caps or pile hats. The national patch was worn on the right shoulder, with a miniature enamelled version on the left collar point;

Mr F. J. Kranenburg, State Secretary for Defence, visits the Netherlands Bn. in Korea, August 1953; at left, the battalion commander, Lt.Col. C. Knulst. (Mil.Hist.Sec., Royal Dutch Army)

the US 2nd Infantry Division's large 'Indian Head' patch was worn on the left shoulder, with a similar miniature on the right collar point; and the US 38th Infantry Regiment's enamelled badge was worn on the left breast (occasionally on the beret or fatigue cap, too). These devices frequently appeared on the fatigue dress, either separately or in combination. Officers wore their own Dutch stars and bars of rank on collar or shoulder strap loops, but NCOs adopted US rank chevrons. Since this NCO's rank had no US equivalent, the Dutch improvised by cutting the upper chevron off the US sergeant's insignia.

F3: Belgium: Capitaine, 1950

The volunteers initially received standard Belgian battledress, which resembled the British model except that it was greener and had longer collar points. They also received British Denison Smocks (some officers wore these privately bought versions similar in style but with a more distinct, 'wavy edged' camouflage pattern). Web equipment and boots followed the British pattern. They adopted a distinctive brown beret; and a gilt badge incorporating the Belgian lion on a shield with a helmet above, backed by the Walloon battleaxe and Flemish 'goedendag' or ball-and-chain mace, the whole over a scroll lettered 'BELGIUM'. The collar

45

patches were brown edged with yellow. Normal Belgian rank insignia were worn; when in shirtsleeve order officers wore miniature versions of the collar patch on the straps. In Korea the Belgians were issued with US steel helmets, winter clothing such as M43 jackets, parkas and pile caps, and US fatigues for use as summer field dress. However, they continued to wear their distinctive berets and camouflage jackets, together with 'British' items such as knitted 'cap comforters' and olive khaki shirts with pleated breast pockets. The national shield patch was worn on the left shoulder, that of the US 3rd Infantry Division on the right, with gold-on-brown 'BELGIUM' shoulder titles above.

G1: Turkey: Major, 1950

The Turks arrived in Korea wearing their recently adopted battledress uniforms with US-pattern field caps made of the same material, British Mk. 2 steel helmets, leather waist belts and German-pattern ammunition pouches. NCOs and men wore no insignia other than a rough disc in arm-of-service colour (green for infantry, blue for artillery) on the side cap, but officers had collar patches in the same colours (Staff wore red). There was only time to issue them with US weapons and some US M1943 combat clothing before they were thrown into action in November 1950, and most were still wearing their battledress, leather equipment and heavy double-breasted greatcoats when they first met the enemy. Subsequently their field clothing, steel helmets and combat equipment became entirely US in style, but they retained their own insignia[1]. The brigade device (a red spearhead decorated with white stars, worn on the right side of the helmet), and the national badge (the white star and crescent on a red circle worn at the top of the right sleeve) seem to have been introduced during 1951. Generals wore their gilt-and-red rank devices on both shoulder straps and helmet fronts, and had gorget patches on their field uniforms as well.

G2: Ethiopia: Lieutenant, 1951

The Ethiopians arrived wearing 1946-pattern British battledress with US-style canvas gaiters; Imperial Guard collar badges; and pith helmets, on the right side of which was a rectangular patch bearing a green, yellow and red cockade. They were

[1]See Plate C1, MAA 157 Flak Jackets.

soon issued with US field uniforms, wearing the US 7th Division's 'diabolo' patch on their left shoulders; a curved 'ETHIOPIA' shoulder title in red on buff edged with red, yellow and green on the right; and, for parade purposes, a large version of the cockade on the right side of the US steel helmet. Towards the end of the period a rather ornate patch bearing the Lion of Judah was introduced: this was worn beneath the 'ETHIOPIA' sleeve title, and on the left side of the steel helmet with the US 7th Division's insignia on the right. The Guard badge continued to be worn on the collar. The Ethiopians retained their own British-style rank insignia. Usually officers wore their gilt Imperial crowns or six-pointed stars on buff-coloured shoulder loops, but appear to have pinned them to the right hand collars of the strapless US summer fatigues, with the Guard badge on the left. NCOs wore British-style chevrons; WOs, wreathed lions or crowns in brass.

G3: Thailand: Lance-Corporal, 1951

This NCO is wearing a 'variant' version of the US M42 HBT fatigues with single pleated breast and hip pockets. These fatigues were made in relatively small numbers, and worn interchangeably with the normal type in both the US and allied armies. His helmet (soon superseded by the US model) looks very much like the French 'Adrian' pattern, which the Thais had certainly worn up to and during World War II, but it is possible that it was in fact an early Japanese model. It bore a national roundel crest which also formed the basis of the cap badge. Junior NCOs' rank chevrons followed the British system, but were embroidered in yellow or gold on a dark blue-green backing, with the roundel surmounted by a pagoda-like Thai crown above, and worn on the left sleeve only. Senior NCOs wore a gilt bar below one to three upward-pointing chevrons on their shoulder straps; company officers, one to three gold stars; field officers the same, but with the upper star surmounted by a Thai crown. Gilt arm-of-service devices were worn on the right collar, with the unit indicated by combinations of Thai lettering and ordinary numerals on the left. The infantry device was crossed rifles with a four-cartridge clip superimposed.

H: Chinese People's Liberation Army
H1: Soldier, winter dress, 1950

The PLA's quilted cotton winter uniform was both light and warm, though the material was difficult to dry when it became wet. The summer uniform was normally worn underneath for additional insulation. Officers seem sometimes to have worn a single-breasted version. The colour was generally an olive khaki, with a white lining which could be reversed to act as snow camouflage. The cap was made from the same material and faced with fur or pile; it had ear flaps which tied under the chin with tapes. Padded mittens with separate trigger fingers were supposed to form part of this uniform, but many soldiers had either lost or never been issued with these, and tucked their hands inside their sleeves instead. The winter boots were made of stout, fur-lined leather and worn with felt leggings, though many troops seem to have continued to wear the canvas summer shoes. This style of uniform, with its external quilting, was replaced from 1952 onwards by one which had the padding on the inside and looked like a bulkier version of the summer uniform. Equipment was usually restricted to a waist belt with two or three stick grenades and two cotton bandoliers, one containing ammunition, the other rice.

H2: Soldier, summer dress, 1951

The PLA's 'official' summer uniform from about 1949 to 1952 seems to have been a Russian-style blouse with a turn-down collar, three-button chest opening, breast pockets and shirt-type cuffs, worn with long trousers and a peaked cap. However, this only appears to have been issued to selected units; and the summer uniform worn in Korea did not differ very much from that worn by the Chinese Nationalists, except that the older field cap had developed into the shapeless 'Mao cap', and puttees seem to have become obsolete. The footwear consisted of canvas shoes with rope or rubber soles. Although there were no official rank insignia, 'leaders' sometimes wore red or red-and-blue armbands, and some were reported to have had red piping diagonally across their cuffs and on their collars, tunic fronts and trouser seams. After 1952 these uniforms were superseded by a plain single-breasted tunic, trousers and Mao cap in 'Yenan green'. The PLA had inherited large stocks of Japanese steel helmets, but few if any seem to have been issued in Korea. Most of the original Chinese

Lt.Col. Vivario, CO of the Belgian Bn. February 1952–February 1953 (and in 1968 Belgian Armed Forces Commander), meets the commanding general of the US 45th Infantry Division, the 'Thunderbirds'. (Belgian National Defence Ministry)

volunteers carried old Chinese or Japanese bolt action rifles or, like this 'tommy gunner', captured US weapons of World War II vintage.

H3: Officer, service dress, 1952

The Chinese People's Liberation Army prided itself on its egalitarianism, and officers and men were all supposed to wear the same simple and austere uniform. In practice differences of style, cut and material continued to exist. In particular, the officers' tunics commonly had four instead of two pockets, and were made of wool or even silk material as opposed to the men's cotton. The colour continued to vary, but tended towards the harsh, yellowish 'Yenan green' derived from the dyes available in the PLA's home province. In the early days the Chinese Communists had worn cloth red star cap badges: after their victory in the civil war they adopted an enamelled version with gold edging, bearing the Chinese characters for '8-1' (commemorating the PLA's date of formation) in the centre. This does not seem to have been worn in Korea, presumably in order to support the fiction that the Chinese were volunteers rather than a national force. The absence of rank insignia was acceptable in a guerrilla force, but re-equipment with Soviet material led to a steady increase in the professionalism of the officer corps; in 1955 new Soviet-style uniforms and insignia were introduced, only to be abolished again during Mao's 'Cultural Revolution' ten years later.

Notes sur les planches en couleur

A1 Uniforme de campagne de style russe; une version simplifiée avec une poche sur la poitrine et des manchettes unies fut introduite plus tard. Le passepoil rouge autour des épaulettes indiquaient l'armée—le passepoil vert, la police des frontières. L'uniforme avait souvent des coutures en zigzag à la poitrine, à l'épaule et sur le coiffe pour maintenir en place les feuillages de camouflage. L'empoi du casque en acier souviétique était rare. **A2** La blouse fut remplacée plus tard par un modèle croisé à cinq boutons. Il y avait aussi une parka croisée avec des poches obliques de côté; et les officiers portaient des pardessus de style soviétique. **A3** L'inspiration russe de cet uniforme est évidente; des pantalons bleu foncé étaient portés pour la parade, des pantalons kaki en campagne. Seuls les coiffes des officiers avaient des passepoils sur le dessus et des lignes diagonales de chaque côté de l'insigne.

B1 Les uniformes ROK étaient presque identiques aux tenues de l'armée des Etats-Unis. Les soldats portaient une version à col fermé de l'uniforme de cet officier, mais seuls les officiers portaient des insignes indiquant le service. **B2** Au début de la guerre, il y avait un mélange de vêtements de campagne, principalement de vieux modèles américains comme cette veste M41; des uniformes M43 furent plus tard distribués en quantité. **B3** Des tenues de toiles américaines étaient portées l'été, souvent avec des coutures en zigzag du style nord-coréen, et cet uniforme en coton molletonné était porté l'hiver. Les insignes de grade étaient souvent vus sur le casque et la poche de poitrine gauche.

C1 Comme tenue de service d'été, des versions en kaki sable clair de la chemise américaine, des pantalons, une tunique à quatre poches et la blouse 'Ike' ou 'battledress' étaient portés; les vestes n'étant portées que par les officiers et les sous-officiers. **C2** Versions M41 et M42 légèrement différentes des tenues de corvée en 'herringbone twill' qui étaient l'uniforme de combat et la tenue de travail normalement portés en été. **C3** Variation de la tenue de corvée, conçue en 1947 mais distribuée seulement au début des années 1950. Les chevrons de grade de la deuxième guerre mondiale étaient plus populaires que les versions miniatures de 1948–51.

D1 La tenue de corvée M43 de l'armée américaine était la tenue de campagne habituelle par temps froid et elle fut largement distribuée aux contingents ROK et UN. La version M1951 avait des poches se fermant avec des pressions et de grandes poches 'cargo' sur les cuisses. **D2** Tenue d'hiver—parka du style de la deuxième guerre mondiale; les versions M1951 n'avaient que les deux poches obliques de côté. Les *Marines* conservèrent les cuissardes en toile de la deuxième guerre mondiale longtemps après l'armée, et les coréens les surnommèrent 'jambes jaunes'. **D3** Des tenues de corvée américaines rendues plus élégantes par des insignes nationaux étaient portées par de nombreux contingents ONU, souvent avec l'insigne d'épaulette de la division américaine à laquelle ils appartenaient.

E1 Les australiens portaient initialement des tenues exclusivement nationales, et ils reçurent plus tard des tenues d'hiver américaines et même des tenues de combat britanniques et des 'flak vests' américaines encore plus tard. La coiffe et les guêtres étaient généralement conservées. **E2** Les troupes britanniques arrivaient avec une tenue de jungle verte et passaient à la 'battledress' pour le premier hiver. Cette tenue était complétée tout d'abord par les tenues camouflées 'windproof' de 1942, et plus tard par la tenue de combat imperméable verte—appelée par la suite uniforme 'M1958'. **E3** Mélange d'articles faits au Canada, inspiré partiellement par les modèles britanniques et partiellement des modèles américains, caractéristique du contingent canadien.

F1 Le bataillon français portait le béret noir, et les insignes de grade et d'unité français avec un uniforme qui était principalement américain. Quelques-uns conservent leurs 'smocks' de camouflage M1942, de confection britannique—la 'peau de saucisse'. La même tenue de camouflage 'windproof' fut distribuée à quelques troupes britanniques et du Commonwealth. **F2** Un uniforme d'inspiration britannique, béret et insignes hollandais, avec quelques uniformes de corvée américains et équipements américains pour le bataillon des Pays-Bas. Des insignes de la 38e régiment d'infanterie et de la 2e division américaines étaient aussi portés. **F3** Un béret brun était portée avec 'battledress', 'Denison smock' et équipement britanniques.

G1 Initialement, les turcs portaient un mélange hétérogène de styles de tenues et d'équipements britanniques, américains et allemands; plus tard, davantage d'éléments américains furent distribués. **G2** Un mélange de tenues et d'équipements britanniques et américains, avec des insignes éthiopiens, fut plus tard remplacé par un uniforme de combat américain, avec les insignes de la 7e division américaine. **G3** Une variante thaïlandaise du casque français Adrian fut portée tout d'abord et elle fut ensuite remplacée part le casque américain. L'uniforme était une version locale de la tenue de corvée américaine M42.

H1 Cet uniforme était reversible—vert d'un côté et blanc de l'autre. Il fut remplacé vers 1952 par une tenue matelassée à l'intérieur qui ressemblait à une version plus volumineuse de la tenue d'été. **H2** A part la coiffe 'Mao', la plupart des chinois portaient des tenues de campagne qui ressemblaient un peu à l'ancien uniforme nationaliste chinois dans les débuts de la guerre. Elle fut ultérieurement remplacée par un uniforme de 'vert Yenan'. Des armes chinoises, japonaises, russes et des armes prises sur les américains étaient utilisées. **H3** Les officiers étaient supposés ne porter que le minimum d'insignes mais les uniformes étaient de qualité supérieure et possédaient de petites différences de détail, quatre poches par exemple.

Farbtafeln

A1 Felduniform im russischen Stil: eine vereinfachte Version mit einer Brusttasche und einfachen Manschetten wurde später eingeführt. Der roten Kordeln um die Schulterstreifen verweisen auf die Armee, grüne auf die Grenzwache. Die Uniform hatte häufig Zickzacknähte an der Brust, den Schultern und der Kappe, um Blättartarnung festzuhalten. Der sowjetische Stahlhelm wurde nur selten verwendet. **A2** Die Bluse wurde später durch eine zweireihige Ausführung mit fünf Knöpfen ersetzt. Ausserdem gab es eine zweireihige Parka mit schräg angesetzten Seitentaschen; Offiziere trugen Mäntel im sowjetischen Stil. **A3** Der russische Einfluss ist bei dieser Uniform deutlich: bei Paraden wurden dunkelblaue Hosen oder Halbhosen getragen, khakifarbene in der Felduniform. Nur die Kappen der Offiziere hatten Kordeln um den Scheitel und die Diagonallinien zu beiden Seiten des Abzeichens.

B1 ROK-Uniformen waren fast identisch mit denen der *US Army*. Soldaten hatten eine Ausführung der Offiziersuniform mit geschlossenem Kragen; nur Offiziere trugen Abzeichen der Waffengattungen. **B2** Zu Beginn des Krieges wurde eine Mischung aus Feldbekleidung getragen, meist obsolete US-Muster wie bei dieser M41 Jacke; M43 Uniformen wurden erst später in grösseren Mengen ausgegeben. **B3** US Drillanzüge wurden im Sommer getragen, mit den nordkoreanischen Zickzacknähten; für den Winter diente diese gesteppte Baumwolluniform. Rangabzeichen fanden sich häufig am Helm und auf der linken Brusttasche.

C1 Als Sommeruniform wurden helle sandfarbene Ausführungen des US Army Hemds, der Hosen, der viertaschigen Jacke und der *Ike* oder *Battledress* Bluse getragen, die Jacken nur von Offizieren und Feldwebeln. **C2** Etwas unterschiedliche M41 und M42 Muster der *Herringbone Twill* Drillanzüge waren die normale Sommerarbeits- und Kampfuniform. **C3** Eine Variation des Drillanzugs, 1947 entworfen, aber erst in den frühen 50er Jahren ausgegeben. Die Rangwinkel aus dem Zweiten Weltkrieg waren populärer als die Miniaturausführungen von 1948–51.

D1 Die M43 Drillanzüge der *US Army* waren die üblichen Felduniformen bei kaltem Wetter und wurden von den Kontingenten der ROK und UN Kontingente häufig benutzt. Die M9151 Version hatte Taschen mit Druckknöpfen und grosse 'Cargo'-Taschen an den Schenkeln. **D2** Winteruniform mit der Parka aus dem Zweiten Weltkrieg; die M1951 Version hatte nur die beiden schrägen Seitentaschen. Die *Marines* behielten noch länger als die Army die Kanvas-Beinschützer des Zweiten Weltkriegs und wurden von den Koreanern mit dem Spitznamen 'Gelbbeiner' bedacht. **D3** 'Elegantere' US Drilluniform mit Landesabzeichen, von vielen UN Kontingenten getragen, oft mit den Schulterabzeichen der dazugehörigen US Division.

E1 Zunächst trugen die Australier landeseigene Bekleidung und erhielten erst später die Winterausrüstung der US Truppen, dann britische Kampuniformen und US 'Flak Vests'. Kopfbedeckung und Gamaschen wurden gewöhnlich beibehalten. **E2** Britische Truppen kamen mit grüner Dschungelbekleidung und übernahmen *Battledress* für den ersten Winter, dazu zunächst 'windproof' Tarnjacken von 1942 und später grüne, abgedichtete Kampuniform (später als 'M1958' bezeichnet). **E3** Eine Mischung aus kanadischen Teilen, die teils durch britische, teils amerikanische Modelle angeregt wurde, war für die kanadische Kontingente typisch.

F1 Das französische Bataillon trug das schwarze Barrett und die französischer Rang- und Einheitsabzeichen meist mit amerikanischen Uniformen. **F2** Durch englische Modelle angeregte Uniform und holländisches Barret und Abzeichen gemeinsam mit einigen US Drillanzügen und Ausrüstungsgegenständen, wurde vom niederländischen Bataillon getragen. Abzeichen der US *38th Infantry* und *2n Division* fanden sich ebenfalls. **F3** Ein braunes Barrett wurde mit dem 'battledress', 'Denison smocks' und Ausrüstung getragen.

G1 Zunächst trugen die Türken eine bunte Mischung aus britischer amerikanischen und deutschen Bekleidungs- und Ausrüstungsgegenständen später wurden mehr US Artikel ausgegeben. **E2** Eine Mischung aus amerikanischer und britischer Bekleidung und Ausrüstung mit äthiopischen Abzeichen, wurde später durch US Kampfuniform abgelöst, die Abzeichen der US *7th Division* trugen. **G3** Eine thailändische Variante des französischen 'Adrian' Helms wurde später durch den US Helm ersetzt. Die Uniform war eine lokale Variante des US M42 Drillanzugs.

H1 Die Uniform konnte umgekehrt werden, mit grüner Innen- und weisse Aussenseite. Ca. 1952 wurde sie durch eine Ausführung mit gesteppter Innenseite ersetzt, die wie eine klobigere Ausführung der Sommeruniform aussah. **H2** Abgesehen von der 'Mao-Mütze' trugen die meisten Chinesen Felduniformen die der alten nationalchinesischen Ausführung der Anfangszeit nicht unähnlich war. Diese Ausführung wurde später durch eine Uniform in 'Yenan-grün' ersetzt. Chinesische, japanische, russische und erbeutete amerikanische Waffen wurden benutzt. **H3** Offiziere sollten nur minimale militärische Abzeichen tragen, dafür waren die Uniformen von höherer Qualität und hatten kleine Unterschiede im Detail, z.B. vier Taschen.